EZ FLASH 5

SHORT PROJECTS AND CREATIVE IDEAS USING MACROMEDIA FLASH

BRADLEY KALDAHL

National Library of Canada Cataloguing in Publication Data

Kaldahl, Bradley, 1961-
  EZ Flash 5

  ISBN 1-55212-899-7

  1. Flash (Computer file) 2. Computer animation. I. Title.
II. Title: Easy Flash five.
TR897.7.K34 2001   006.6'96   C2001-911267-X

TRAFFORD

This book was published *on-demand* in cooperation with Trafford Publishing.
On-demand publishing is a unique process and service of making a book available for retail sale to the public taking advantage of on-demand manufacturing and Internet marketing.
On-demand publishing includes promotions, retail sales, manufacturing, order fulfilment, accounting and collecting royalties on behalf of the author.

Suite 6E, 2333 Government St., Victoria, B.C. V8T 4P4, CANADA
Phone   250-383-6864   Toll-free   1-888-232-4444 (Canada & US)
Fax   250-383-6804   E-mail   sales@trafford.com
Web site www.trafford.com   TRAFFORD PUBLISHING IS A DIVISION OF TRAFFORD HOLDINGS LTD.
Trafford Catalogue #01-0301   www.trafford.com/robots/01-0301.html

10   9   8   7   6   5   4   3   2   1

Dedication
To my 3 year old daughter Sam.
My inspiration, who's smile brightens every day.
You have demonstrated more courage and strength
than most are required to exhibit in a lifetime.
I am lucky to have such a wonderful daughter.
Dad

Acknowledgments:
Thanks to my spouse Sonia, for the late night visits to the office to print proof copies, for understanding when I came to bed while you were getting up, and for the support you have demonstrated in so many other ways (I really am a lucky fellow).
Fred Howell, (my dept. chair) and a great friend. I could not have written this without your dedication and support. (I am also forever in your debt for the schedule accommodations.)
George Payne (Vice President). George you have a magic gift with people. As always thank you for your unwavering support and guidance.
Ed Roberts (Dean) The true Mac techno guru. You always seem to have the info I need.
Alan Vincent, Friend, colleague, techno wizard, and ski buddy. (I still have your gloves)
To friends and colleagues who continue to captivate me with their knowledge and expertise.
Helen Youth, Sue Liggett, Sandy Ridgly, Mike Cantwell, Mike O'Conner and too many others to mention in this short space.
To my friends (who have far more professional experience with book publishing than I) and were so kind to edit and advise Jackie Mintz and Wilda Anderson. So many of your comments and suggestions helped to make this text a much better product. In my haste to get this book into production I know I've missed some of your corrections, so I must take the blame for errors.
Jacob Kirk my teaching assistant. Your enthusiasm is contagious. Your comments, suggestions and ideas invaluable.
Ray Kimbell and Ann Johnson for your creative ideas, enthusiasm and support.
A special thanks to my students. While I am employed to educate, I always find that I receive far more than I am able to give. Your creativity (sometime to the point of bizarre), willingness to explore and to push the limits of this new technology amazes and thrills me.
To see selected examples of students work go to HotFlashBook.com and select the student examples link.

Condensed Table of Contents

Introduction

1. About the Book 1

Flash Interface

2. Introduction to Flash 9
3. Flash Palettes 19

Symbols and Tweening

4. Symbols & Tweening 23
5. Melting Shapes 29
6. Melting Type Animation **33**
7. Solar Explosion 37
8. Spinning Text 45

Layers

9. Layers 49
10. Explosion Using Layers 55

Publishing

11. Publishing Flash on the Web 61

Buttons

12. Interactivity with Buttons 67
13. Connecting to the Web 75
14. Controlling Animation with ActionScript 79
15. Interactive Web Portfolio with ActionScript 85

Sounds

16. Sound & Buttons 95

17. Controlling MP3 Sound With Flash 97

18. Controlling MP3 Sounds with ActionScript 105

Movie Clips

19. Interactive MovieClips 113

20. Interactive Web Game 119

21. Web Paint, Reverse Engineering Flash Web Content 127

22. Interactive Web for Photographers 135

ActionScript and Text Fields

23. Dynamic Text Fields 143

24. Animated Typist 149

Preloaders and Download Testing

25. Flash Preloading 153

26. Download Testing 157

Animation Paths and Trails

27. Path Animation 161

28. Animated Motion Trails 167

Advanced ActionScript

29. Collision Testing, Score Keeping & Dragging Objects 171

Using other Applications with Flash

30. Using Photoshop with Flash 181

31. Using Illustrator with Flash 187

Final Tips & Suggestions

32. Final Tips & Suggestions 193

Contents

Chapter 1 1

  How Flash is Different From other Web Applications . 1

  Imbedding Animations within Animations 2

  Features Compared to other Web Applications 2

  Flash vs Animated GIF's 3

  Flash vs Java & JavaScript 3

  Flash vs DreamWeaver & GoLive 3

  Other Web Animation Technologies 3

  Animation without Plug-ins 3

  Scripting 4

  Better than Flash 4

  Powerful Programing Effects Without Programing 4

  Is This Book Right For Your? 5

  New Flash Users 5

  Experienced Flash Users 5

  Skills Needed to Learn Flash 6

  Ways to Approach Flash 6

  Helpful Skills 6

  The Structure of this Book 7

  Sections 7

  Chapters 7

  Action Steps 8

  Learning ActionScript 8

SECTION I FLASH INTERFACE

INTRODUCTION TO FLASH

Chapter 2 9

  Animation Basics 11

  Frame by Frame animation 11

  First Animation Project 12

  The Tool Palette 12

  Inserting Keyframes 13

CREATING MOVEMENT 13

DRAWING ON THE STAGE 13

PLAYING THE ANIMATION 14

STOP ANIMATION FROM PLAYING 14

CREATING THE BOUNCE 15

RESIZING AN OBJECT OVER TIME 15

ONION SKIN 16

EXAGGERATION ADDS INTEREST 17

FURTHER EXPLORATION 18

CREATING THE ILLUSION OF IMPACT. 18

FLASH PALETTES

Chapter 3 19

INFO PALETTE 19

TRANSFORM PALETTE 20

STROKE PALETTE 20

FILL PALETTE 20

CHANGING GRADIENT SETTINGS 21

APPLYING A GRADIENT WITH THE PAINT BUCKET 21

FURTHER EXPLORATION 22

IMPORTING PHOTOSHOP IMAGES INTO FLASH 22

SECTION 2 TWEENING

SYMBOLS   TWEENING

Chapter 4 23

CREATING A GRAPHIC SYMBOL 24

LIBRARY PALETTE 25

SYMBOL EDITOR 25

WHAT HAPPENED! MY ANIMATION VANISHED 25

TWEENING 26

THE FRAME PALETTE 26

FADING OVER TIME 27

SAVE EVERYTHING 27

EXPERIMENTING WITH TWEENING 27

REVIEW QUESTIONS 28

ADDITIONAL EXPERIMENTATION 28

Chapter 5 29
    Shape Tween 29
    Pencil Tool Options 30
    What is a Blank Keyframe? 30
    KeyFrame Shortcuts 30
    Tween/Frame Palette 31
    Shape vs. Motion Tween 32

MELTING TYPE ANIMATION

Chapter 6 .... **33**
    Shape Tweened Type 33
    Setup 33
    The Character Palette 34
    Turning Text into a Graphic 35
    Type Tweening Tips 36

SOLAR EXPLOSION

Chapter 7 37
    Topics 37
    Setup 37
    Setting the Line to None 38
    Changing Gradient Settings 38
    Creating a Graphic Symbol 39
    Resizing a Graphic 40
    Creating the Explosion 40
    Resizing the Stage 41
    Making an Object Grow Larger Than the Stage 41
    Creating a Motion Tween 42
    Special Effects with Skewing 43
    Resizing the Movie 43
    Closing the Test Movie 43
    Testing the Movie in a Separate Window. 43
    Changing Animation Speed 44

Chapter 8 45

 SETUP.. 45

 CHARACTER ATTRIBUTES 46

 MOTION TWEEN 46

 EASING IN AND EASING OUT 47

 CHANGING AN OBJECTS CENTER POINT 47

 ADDITIONAL EXPERIMENTATION 48

SECTION 3 LAYERS

LAYERS

Chapter 9 49

 FLASH LAYERS 49

 PROJECT

 SETUP - REVIEW 50

 ADDING NEW LAYERS 51

 HIDING A LAYER 51

 SECOND ANIMATION ON A NEW LAYER 51

 NAMING LAYERS 51

 LOCKING A LAYER 51

 CREATING A SEPARATE ANIMATION ON LAYER 2 52

 SYMBOL EDITOR PROBLEMS 52

 MOTION TWEEN ON LAYER 2 53

 UNLOCKING A LAYER 53

 FURTHER EXPLORATION 54

EXPLOSION USING LAYERS

Chapter 10 55

 LAYER ANIMATION

 MOTION TWEENED EXPLOSION 55

 USING THE LASSO TOOL 56

 SELECT THE LAYER BEFORE DRAGGING A SYMBOL 57

 EACH LAYER SHOULD CONTAIN ONE PIECE OF THE BALL . 57

 SYMBOLS REMAIN IN THE LIBRARY PALETTE 57

 REASSEMBLE THE CIRCLE 58

 CREATING KEYFRAMES ON SEVERAL LAYERS AT ONCE. 58

WHAT IS AN IN-BETWEEN FRAME? 59
PROJECT SUMMARY 59
FURTHER EXPLORATION INTRODUCTION TO ACTIONSCRIPT ... 60

SECTION 4 PUBLISHING

Chapter 11 61

EXPORTING & SAVING FOR THE WEB 61
PUBLISH SWF FILES FOR DISTRIBUTION ON THE WEB. 62
PUBLISH OPTIONS 62
FLASH EXPORT SETTINGS 63
MP3 SOUND 63
PUBLISHING TO AN OLDER VERSION OF FLASH 63
HTML SETTINGS 64
CREATING A FULL PAGE WEB SITE WITH FLASH 64
JUST A COUPLE OF CLICKS AND ITS READY FOR THE WEB 65
EXPORTING FLASH USING THE ANIMATED GIF FORMAT 65
ANIMATED GIF FEATURES 66
USING FLASH HELP 66

SECTION 5 BUTTONS

INTERACTIVITY WITH BUTTONS

Chapter 12 67

BUTTONS CAN CHANGE THE ENTIRE STAGE 67
THE SECRET OF FLASH 67
BUTTON OBJECTS ARE ESSENTIAL FOR CREATING GAMES. ... 68
PROJECT 69
CONVERTING AN OBJECT INTO A BUTTON SYMBOL 69
ENTERING THE BUTTON SYMBOL EDITOR 70
FLASH BUTTON STATES 70
ADDING A BLANK KEYFRAMES TO CREATE BUTTON STATES 71
TESTING THE BUTTON 71
CREATING AN OVER STATE. 71
CREATING A DOWN STATE. 72
ADDING A KEYFRAMES TO CREATE BUTTON STATES 72
SAVE THIS PROJECT IT WILL BE USED IN THE NEXT SECTION ... 72

THE HIT STATE 73

FURTHER EXPLORATION 74

Chapter 13 75

OBJECT ACTIONS WINDOW 76

CAPTURING MOUSE EVENTS 76

CONNECT TO WEB PAGE ACTION 77

WHERE CAN ACTIONSCRIPTS BE APPLIED? 77

LINKING TO PAGES LOCALLY 77

ADDITIONAL EXPERIMENTATION 78

PREVIEW IN BROWSER 78

CONTROLLING ANIMATION WITH ACTIONSCRIPT

Chapter 14 79

ABOUT THIS PROJECT 79

SETUP 79

CREATING A BUTTON SYMBOL 80

ACCESSING ACTIONSCRIPT 80

CREATING A STOP SCRIPT 81

VIEWING THE SCRIPT 81

TESTING THE SCRIPT 81

ADDING INSTANCES OF THE MASTER BUTTON 82

CREATING A PLAY SCRIPT 82

SCRIPTING THE RESTART BUTTON WITH GOTO 83

GOTO SCRIPT OPTIONS 83

FURTHER EXPLORATION 84

INTERACTIVE WEB PORTFOLIO WITH ACTIONSCRIPT

Chapter 15 85

THE PROJECT 85

CREATING THE INTRO SCENE 86

ZOOMING TYPE 86

ADDING USER NAVIGATION 87

INSERT DUMMY IMAGES 87

CREATING THE MASTER BUTTON SYMBOL 88

SEGMENTING THE MOVIE 88

ADDING NAVIGATION SCRIPTS TO THE BUTTONS 88

GO TO AND STOP SCRIPT 89

SCRIPTING THE SECOND BUTTON 89

CREATING A RETURN BUTTON 90

ADDING A SCRIPTED BUTTON TO THE LIBRARY 91

REUSING A BUTTON SYMBOL.. 92

ADDING FRAME ACTIONS 93

TEST THE MOVIE 94

FURTHER EXPLORATION 94

SECTION 6 SOUNDS

SOUND BUTTONS

Chapter 16 95

SOUND IMPORT PROBLEMS 96

TESTING SOUNDS IN FLASH 96

ADDING SOUND TO THE OVER STATE 96

ADDING SOUND TO THE DOWN STATE 96

CONTROLLING MP3 SOUND WITH FLASH

Chapter 17 97

WHY USE FLASH FOR BACKGROUND SOUNDS? 97

CONCEPTS COVERED 98

ABOUT PROGRAMMING IN FLASH 98

COPYRIGHT ISSUES WITH SOUNDS 99

THE PROJECT 99

FINDING COPYRIGHT FREE SOUNDS 99

PROJECT SET-UP 100

SIMPLE ROLLOVER EFFECT FOR PNG IMAGE 101

ADDING SOUND TO THE DOCUMENT: 102

ACCESSING FLASH INSTANCE SCRIPTING 103

STOP ALL SOUNDS SCRIPT 103

FURTHER EXPLORATION 104

Chapter 18 105

PROJECT SETUP 105

SETUP CONTINUED 106

LINKING A LIBRARY SOUND FOR USE BY ACTIONSCRIPT.... 107

LINKAGE IDENTIFIER 107

THE PROJECT 107

CREATING THE SOUND-OFF BEHAVIOR 108

THE STOP SOUND SCRIPT 108

SCRIPTING THE ON BUTTON 109

ACTIONSCRIPT TO PLAY LINKED LIBRARY SOUND............ 109

DISSECTING THE CODE 110

SECTION 7 MOVIE CLIPS

INTERACTIVE MOVIECLIPS

Chapter 19 113

ADDING ACTION SCRIPT 114

SCRIPT VIEW 114

ADDING A SECOND EVENT SCRIPT TO THE BUTTON 115

MODIFYING AN EVENT SCRIPT 115

SAVE THIS MOVIE 116

CONVERTING A BUTTON ANIMATION INTO A MOVIECLIP 116

SELECTING ALL FRAMES IN A MOVIE 116

COPYING AN ANIMATION 116

CREATE A MOVIECLIP SYMBOL 117

PASTE THE COPIED FRAMES INTO THE MOVIECLIP SYMBOL 117

USING THE MOVIECLIP IN A NEW MOVIE 118

FURTHER EXPERIMENTATION 118

INTERACTIVE WEB GAME

Chapter 20 119

THE PROJECT 120

ADDING BUTTON STATES 120

OVER STATE GUN SITES 121

DOWN STATE EXPLOSION 121

ADDING THE BUTTON SOUND 122
EDITING ACTIONSCRIPT 123
ACTIONSCRIPT TO MAKE THE BUTTON VANISH 123
CREATING THE MOVIECLIP 124
FURTHER EXPLORATION 125
USING THE MOVIE CLIP IN A NEW ANIMATION 125
FURTHER EXPLORATION 126

WEB PAINT REVERSE ENGINEERING FLASH WEB CONTENT

Chapter 21 127
FLASH QUIZ PROJECT 127
FLASH EXPERT 131

INTERACTIVE WEB FOR PHOTOGRAPHERS

Chapter 22 135
SCREEN SHOT EXAMPLE 135
PROJECT OVERVIEW 136
RELATED PROJECTS 136
CREATE THE BUTTON 137
PROJECT SETUP 137
CREATE THE TWEEN 137
CREATE FRAME CONTROL 138
ADD THE BUTTON CONTROL 139
CREATING THE MOVIE CLIP 140
CREATING THE FINAL ANIMATION 140
ADDING THE MOVIE CLIPS 141
FURTHER EXPLORATION 142

SECTION 8 ACTION FIELDS

Chapter 23 143

IMPORTANT TERMINOLOGY BASICS 143

VARIABLES 144

NUMERIC VARIABLES 144

TEXT VARIABLES 144

CREATING TEXT STRINGS 145

ACQUIRING PROGRAMMING SKILLS 145

THE LOOP COUNTER PROJECT: 146

CREATING DYNAMIC TEXT 146

ADDING A CONTROL LAYER 147

ADD A TIMER TO YOUR WEB GAME PROJECT. 148

USING IF STATEMENTS 148

ANIMATED TYPIST

Chapter 24 149

THE PROJECT 149

SETTING UP THE TEXT FIELD 150

ADDING THE SCRIPTING LAYER 150

CREATING THE SCRIPT 151

COPY AND PASTE A SCRIPT 151

FURTHER EXPLORATION 152

SECTION 9 PRELOAD TESTING

FLASH PRELOADING

Chapter 25 153

WHAT IS A PRELOAD MOVIE 153

STREAMING MEDIA 153

WHAT TO INCLUDE IN A PRELOADER 153

THE PROJECT 154

Q&A ABOUT PRELOADERS 156

FURTHER EXPERIMENTATION 156

Chapter 26 157
    TESTING A FLASH MOVIE AT DIFFERENT CONNECTION SPEEDS 157
    PROJECT 158
    FLASH MOVIE PLAYBACK OPTIONS 158

SECT.10 ANIMATION TRAILS

PATH ANIMATION

Chapter 27 161
    THE PROJECT 161
    CREATE THE FRAMES BUT WAIT ON THE TWEEN 162
    USE THE PENCIL TOOL ON FRAME 1 OF THE GUIDE LAYER 163
    APPLY THE TWEEN TO OBJECT LAYER 163
    ALIGN THE OBJECT TO THE MOTION PATH 164
    ADDITIONAL EXPLORATION 165
    SAVE AS A MOVIECLIP FOR THE NEXT CHAPTER 165
    PATH BASED SUMMARY 166

ANIMATED MOTION TRAILS

Chapter 28 167
    MOTION TRAILS 167
    PROJECT 168
    USE MULTIPLE COPIES OF THE MOVIECLIP 169

SECT.11 MORE ACTIONSCRIPT

COLLISION TESTING, SCORE KEEPING   DRAGGING OBJECTS

Chapter 29 171
    PROJECT 171
    LETTING THE USER DRAG AN OBJECT 172
    IDEAS FOR DRAG OBJECTS 174
    ANIMATING A DRAGABLE OBJECT 174
    VARIATIONS ON THE SCRIPT 175
    HIT TEST SCRIPT 176
    KEEPING SCORE 176

FINAL SCRIPT 178

SCORE FIELD 179

HIT OBJECT 179

NAMING THE HIT OBJECT 180

12 OTHER APPLICTIONS

USING PHOTOSHOP WITH FLASH

Chapter 30 181

PHOTOSHOP 6.0 AND FLASH 181

THE PROJECT 182

SAVE FOR WEB 184

IMPORTING THE PNG INTO FLASH 185

ADDITIONAL EXPERIMENTATION MELTING HEAD 186

USING ILLUSTRATOR WITH FLASH

Chapter 31 187

USING ILLUSTRATOR 9 WITH FLASH 187

PROJECT 188

ILLUSTRATOR EXPORT OPTIONS 189

SWF FORMAT DIALOG 190

EXPORT OPTIONS 191

IMAGE OPTIONS 191

IMPORTING ILLUSTRATOR INTO FLASH 191

FURTHER EXPLORATION: 192

FINAL TIPS SUGGESTIONS

Chapter 32 193

HANDLING BIG PROJECTS 193

FURTHER READING 195

THE COMMUNICATION REVOLUTION 196

Note to Readers:
Flash offers web capability like no application before. Flash has become the application of choice by the most creative and experimental web designers. Learning how to use Flash should not be frustrating but instead should be liberating. As a professional Flash trainer I designed this book to take you step by step into the most exciting features of Flash and to make the learning process as enjoyable as possible. While the projects may take only 15- 30 minutes to complete I hope you will take the time to try some of the additional experimentation suggestions at the end of many of the projects.

To access some of the source files used in this book log onto **http://hotFlashBook.com**

Note to Educators:
I am sure my friends and colleagues will find this text ideal for classroom use. I could not find the Flash materials that I felt would best introduce new students as well as captivate experienced students. I started writing short projects to illustrate features and techniques in Flash and was delighted by the positive student response. Based on praise from students and colleagues I decided to pull these projects together into a text book. As a fellow academic I am sure you will quickly recognize how this text was designed to fit into different academic situations, and appeal to a variety of different learning styles. Because the projects are open ended this text should fit well with any course that utilize Flash including Computer Applications, Visual Arts, Publishing, and of course, Web and Internet design curricula. Additionally, if you have not taught a Flash course before, you will be delighted to find sample syllabi, additional projects, a faculty Q&A page and test questions available at the Educator Only (http://hotflashbook.com) web site. All files on the faculty web site are provided copyright free and available for immediate use in the class, provided you are using the EZ Flash text.

Educators can access course syllabi, course outlines, lecture notes, and a variety of course materials including additional source files for class demonstrations and additional tutorial as they become available. All of these materials are granted copyright free with the provision, of course, that you are using the text in your class. Note: please be aware that I have invested a great deal of time and effort into making this text available. My publisher and I have also tried to insure that this text is as inexpensive as possible. Wether you are teaching a one day seminar or a full semester course I must reiterate that it is copyrighted material and no portion of this book can be reproduced in any way or fashion. On the other hand, all course development materials are granted for free distribution and modification assuming your are using this text for your course.

For course materials please visit http://hotFlashBook.com and select the educator link to obtain instructions on access procedures for the educators web site.

CHAPTER 1

About Flash 5

Topics

Flash vs Web Applications 1
Animations in Animations 2
Features in Common with other
Web Applications 2
Flash vs Animated GIF's 3
Flash vs Java & JavaScript 3
DreamWeaver & GoLive 3
Web Animation Technologies 3
Animation without Plug-ins 3
Scripting 4
Better than Flash 4
Powerful Programing Effects
Without Programing 4
Is This Book Right For You? 5
New Flash Users 5
Experienced Flash Users 5
Skills Needed to Learn Flash 6
Ways to Approach Flash 6
Helpful Skills 6
The Structure of this Book 7
Sections 7
Action Steps 7
Chapters 7
Learning ActionScript 8

Flash has emerged as a powerhouse web interactivity and animation package. Whether you want to create a simple splash screen to add interest to your web page, or use the application to produce your entire web site, Flash offer capabilities and features that cannot be found in any other web production application.

First let's discuss what makes Flash different, then let's explore some of the features Flash has in common with other web tools.

Flash was the first vector-based as opposed to pixel-based web content application.

HOW FLASH IS DIFFERENT FROM OTHER WEB APPLICATIONS

If you create a web page and place a full-screen, full-color Photoshop, or Fireworks, scanned image on the page, it will take a while to download. A vector-based Flash image that is full-screen and full-color will load in a fraction of the time. As you work through the projects in this book, you will gain a better understanding of what vector-based animation is, but for now the key thing to remember is that simple vector images are smaller in file size and can therefore download much faster. You will also note that you can use scanned pixel-based images in Flash, and as this book will show, because of Flash's streaming capabilities, you can create small, fast-loading animations that play while the larger pixel-based images download in the background

IMBEDDING ANIMATIONS WITHIN ANIMATIONS

The second and most dynamic feature about Flash which sets it apart from other web software, is its ability to place an animation inside another animation. About 80 to 90% of the really cool Flash sites on the web take advantage of this capability. As you work through this book, there are tutorials that explore this capability. While placing one animation inside another is relatively easy, the depth and power that this feature provides is overwhelming.

FLASH COMPARED TO OTHER WEB DEVELOPMENT APPLICATIONS

How is Flash different than other Web production applications?

Flash is a powerful animation package with a lot of great features. It has Tweening capabilities which means you do not have to create every frame of the animation. Not only can it produce Tweens for movement but also for size, color, and transparency. Flash also includes a feature that is referred to as Shape Tweening. Shape tweening is similar to morphing but it works with vector drawings. This is not as sophisticated as some of the bitmap morph applications you may have encountered, but it does open a huge doorway into unusual and abstract transitions.

Is Flash the best web animation application available? This all depends upon what you want to create.
If your animation needs are basic, then there are other applications and technologies to choose from.

1. DHTML allows timeline animation and is built into both DreamWeaver and GoLive, no coding required.
2. Animated GIF's can also be used to create simple looping graphics but they do not provide interactivity.
3. The JavaScript, scripting language, allows some cool animated effects but is limited by your programming skills.
4. The Java programming language offers an infinite variety of programming effects but again it is limited by your programming skills.

DHTML, Animated GIF's, JavaScript, and Java, all have one feature that might make them preferable to Flash. They do not require that a plug-in be downloaded and are standard features of both Netscape and Internet Explorer version 4 or later. A simple bit of animation to be displayed as web page "eye candy" might be better using something other than Flash.

If you want interactivity, fast download, and something a little more complex, or interactive, then you will prefer Flash over animated GIF's. Animated GIF's are great for very simple small animated images but larger animated scenes created using the GIF format become unusable because of monstrous download times.

If you already know JavaScript or Java then you know that a simple animation can require hours of programming time not to mention the years of training it may take to master programming concepts. On the other hand, if you already know Java or JavaScript then you will feel right at home with the ActionScript language provided in Flash which is similar to JavaScript.

If you have worked with DreamWeaver or GoLive, I encourage you to explore the animation timeline functions and DHTML. You will be amazed at how these feature correspond to some of the concepts you will learn about in Flash. You may even find ways to incorporate your Flash animation with DHTML animation. Both DreamWeaver and GoLive allow you to incorporate Flash animations into your web pages, and both have behaviors that allow you to check and redirect your user's browser if they do not currently have

Flash Scripting

Powerful Programing Effects Without Programing

Better than Flash

the Flash Plug-in. But, you can also create your entire website using only Flash.

Flash includes a scripting language similar to JavaScript. If you are not familiar with programming, then Flash is a wonderful way to begin to learn basic programming concepts. With Flash you can focus most of your attention on creating graphics, animations, and scenes and then enhance the animation with a few scripts. You could also, go all out with Action Script and create highly interactive content. One important thing to be aware of is with Flash you can create powerful interactive web content with no scripting or with just a minimum of scripting. Some of the most powerful pieces I see on the web use very little scripting and rely instead on Flash's ability to imbed animations inside animations.

Believe it or not, Flash is not the only graphical tool for interactive web production. Flash allows the production of small (in file size), fast downloading, entertaining and interactive web animations. As you learn Flash you will find that there are things you want to do that Flash cannot. When you reach this point, you are ready to take the next step into the big guns of interactive web development. Flash has a big brother (or sister) that has been around longer than Netscape, Internet Explorer or even Mosaic: Macromedia Director. The great thing about Flash is that while you are learning it you are also becoming familiar with other Macromedia products, including Director. After you have completed the projects in this text, look for my next book, which will have a similar layout and focus on the power user interactive web features found in Macromedia Director.

If you have previous experience with Flash, you will find this book to be an excellent resource for ideas. I'm sure you will enjoy the clear organization of topics, and the variety of experimental ideas presented in short (2-8 page), easy to follow, hands-on format. This book contains more than 30 short projects and over 100 ideas that cover a variety of effects such as Melting Type, Solar Explosions, Animated Typist, Fast and Easy Web Games, Sound Controllers, Interactive Web Photographs, Fading Web Paint, Spinning Type, and Web Portfolios. There is a section on how to reverse engineer interesting web content for use in your own creations and a section on creating and testing preloaders. Additionally, this text provides a straight-forward introduction to ActionScript.

Because this book is designed for newcomers as well as experienced Flash users, you will find the information clearly presented in a way that allows you create the desired effect fast and easy.

New Flash Users

If you have never worked with Flash you will appreciate the easy-to-use, short, step by step projects. Rather than reading about each palette and menu item to find out what they do, you will learn by doing. From the second chapter on, you will be quickly producing exciting web content, while exploring the Flash interface.

As an educator I designed this text because I could find no books that provide the beginner with a logical, easy to understand, progression for learning Flash in a hands-on format. Both my students and I agree that the most enjoyable way to learn complex software is with short projects that show cool, fun, interesting techniques that can be used (or modified) immediately.

Each chapter not only offers interesting projects but also builds on the previous chapter. Many chapters include additional suggestions and ideas, at the end of the chapter. These additional experimentation projects discuss different ways the chapter concepts can be applied to create exciting new content. By experimenting you will also improve your knowledge and skill with Flash.

If you are in a hurry to learn Flash, then you could quickly work through the first project in each chapter in order to get the skills needed for the Power User Flash features discussed in later chapters, but you would be missing out on some really cool projects along the way.

These projects have been classroom tested, and modified, based on student questions, to insure that you will find learning Flash both enjoyable and easy to understand. Extensive screen shots means that you can learn much of this application simply by looking at the diagrams. Short 2-8 page projects means that you can focus on a specific concept before moving onto the next.

Skills Needed to Learn Flash

Flash is not designed for the computer novice. If you have less than 6 month's experience on the computer then I urge you to look for other books or courses that may better prepare you for working with Flash. This book is designed for individuals with basic computer skills and a desire to learn how to create interactivity and animation for the web. This book will not teach you how to navigate on a computer, nor will it teach you how to upload your files to the web, or how to set up a web site with your ISP (Internet Service Provider). Those are topics for other books or can be answered by your ISP.

Helpful Skills

It is not required but it can be helpful to have some knowledge of Photoshop or Fireworks to manipulate scanned images, Illustrator or Freehand, to create vector graphics, and sound utilities to capture and modify sound samples. Flash 5 also accepts quicktime video. As you will see in this book, these skills are not required, but after (or while) learning Flash, you may want to explore these other applications.

Ways to Approach Flash

There are a couple of ways to approach Flash. The first is to come up with the most creative ideas possible and then try to see if you can force Flash to produce the idea. This can be fun once you know Flash but frustrating if you are new to Flash because Flash has very finite limits to what it can do.

The second approach, and the one that I strongly endorse, if you are new to Flash, is to first discover what Flash can do by using this book. Then experiment with Flash to gain a better understanding of what you can make it do. During the discovery process you will come up with some great ideas, jot them down so you can come back to them later. Then knowing what Flash can do, push yourself to think "outside the box" of every other Flash web site you have seen. Explore and develop creative uses for Flash that no one has ever thought of before.

By working through these projects you will gain much more insight into Flash than could be obtained from simply reading. I believe the best way to learn is to first get comfortable with the tool then experiment with your own ideas to become expert.

I have tried to keep each section and chapter tightly focused on a single concept, and I have paired down the concept to the essentials. At the beginning of each section you will work with simple objects. As you work through the project, think about how you could expand the concept using more interesting graphics and images. The real fun begins when you start to apply this tool and these concepts to your own creative ideas.

The sections are designed to produce an easy progression into Flash. After an introduction to Flash and basic animation concepts, the next section explores Symbols and Tweening. Subsequent sections explore Layers, Buttons, and MovieClips. To gain the most from Flash you ultimately want to have a solid understanding of MovieClips but to start with MovieClips would cause frustration since the content from the previous sections is essential to make the most of MovieClips. Each section provides several projects to help reinforce the skill and to explore alternative ways that the section topic can be used in Flash.

At the end of each chapter you will find suggestions for further experimentation. To really understand Flash and to gain some insight into how the concept can be used I encourage you to try the "further experimentation".

THE STRUCTURE OF THIS BOOK

SECTIONS

CHAPTERS

ACTION STEPS

This is a hands-on learning text. While projects may include short explanations of key concepts you need to know the majority of the content is hands-on Action Steps.

Throughout this book, all "action-steps" will have a checkbox ❏ in front. I encourage you to check off the steps as you go and to make notes in the margin to remind you of specific procedures.

LEARNING ACTIONSCRIPT

This text will gradually introduce the scripting language, ActionScript. By the time you reach the later chapters, that focus on ActionScript, you should be comfortable with scripting in Flash.

Scripting is shown in the courier typeface to set it apart from the other text of this book.

for example....

```
on (rollOver) {
  gotoAndPlay (1);
}
```

Previous experience with scripting or programming, will be helpful as you dig further into Flash. The Syntax and structure of the scripting language is similar to JavaScript and Visual Basic. If you are expereinced, you may prefer using the expert mode, which allows manually entry of your scripts.

If you have no experience with scripting, or a fear of scripting, then you will really enjoy working with Flash. By working with Flash in the normal mode, the application will enter the scripts for you based on menu selections, then provide options that you can modify with a click of a button. I personally believe that applications like Flash provide the most painless and enjoyable introduction to computer programming.

This chapter explores some of the basic features of Flash. Rather than reading a dry discourse, you will work with Flash to create your first animation while learning the layout of the application. This project will expose you to the tool palette, stage, timeline, and other palettes in Flash. In addition to learning some of the tools and palettes, the most important benefit is to gain comfort with the use of a timeline. The biggest obstacle most novice animators encounter when working with an animation timeline are the concepts of frames and keyframes. Once you understand what a keyframe is and how to add one to the timeline the rest of Flash becomes much easier to understand.

Let's Begin!

❏ Launch Flash 5.0

❏ Choose the menu command Window-Panel Sets-Default Layout.
This will reset all of the palettes to their default locations.

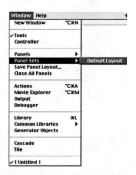

Topics

The Project 10
Frame by Frame Animation 11
Animation Basics 11
The Tool Palette 12
First Animation Project 12
Creating Movement 13
Inserting Keyframes 13
Drawing on the Stage 13
Playing the Animation 14
Stop Animation from Playing ... 14
Creating the Bounce 14
Resizing an Object Over Time   15
Onion skin 16
Exaggeration Adds Interest 17
Further Exploration 18
Creating the Illusion of Impact. 18

First Look Around:

With all of the palettes reset to their default locations your monitor screen should resemble the diagram displayed at the bottom of this page.

The main window contains both the timeline and the stage. The tool palette (on the left) displays a variety of tools, I'm sure you can guess at the use of some of them simply by looking at the icon. Options for each tool are displayed either on the lower half of the tool palette or on the other palettes displayed on the right side of your monitor.

The main window contains two different areas. The upper half displays the timeline. It allows you to create movement over time for animation.

Below the timeline is the stage. This is the area where animation takes place and represents what the user will see. This is also the area where you will draw, position, and create your animation.

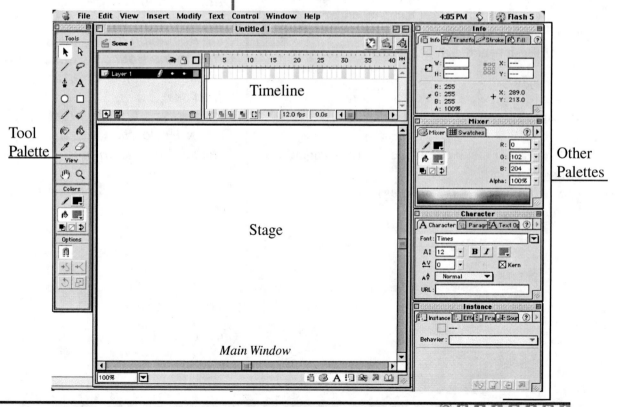

Tool Palette

Other Palettes

Timeline

Stage

Main Window

Animation Basics

One way to create a simple animation would be to use a notepad or even this book.

Lets say that on the first page of this book you drew a circle at the bottom of the page. Then on the next facing page you drew the exact same circle but moved it up a little. Then, on the next page you moved it further up and so on until you reached the last page where the circle was at the top of the page. If you flipped through the pages rapidly the circle would appear to move or would appear to be animated.

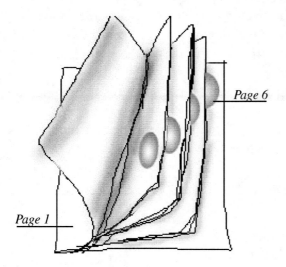

Page 6

Page 1

Flash works on the same principle. To create the same animation in Flash we would start with frame 1. Frame number 1 of the timeline could be thought of as page 1, so we place a circle at the bottom of the stage. Frame number 2 on the timeline would represent page number 2, so we move the circle a little closer to the top of the stage. With each frame we move the circle closer to the top until we reach a frame where the circle is at the top of the stage. Then, when we play the animation back, we are

FRAME BY FRAME ANIMATION

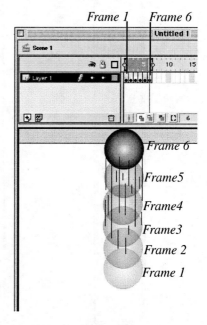

Frame 1   Frame 6

Frame 6
Frame 5
Frame 4
Frame 3
Frame 2
Frame 1

seeing the illusion of the object moving from the bottom to the top of the stage.

So each frame of the timeline represents the page numbers or one small point in time of the movement of our animation. The stage is the place that we create the animation and see it in action.

Your first animation project:

The purpose of this project is to experiment with the timeline in Flash and produce a simple frame by frame animation of a bouncing ball. This will also give you an opportunity to explore some of the basic procedures used in Flash. For the first part of this project you will create a 5-frame animation where a ball begins in the center of the stage then moves (frame by frame) to the right.

❑ Launch Flash, if it is not already running.

❑ Choose Window-Palette Sets-Default Layout to reset the palettes.

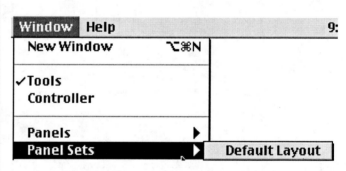

This sets all of the palettes to their default position. At the beginning of each project I will ask you to do this so your screen matches the screen shots used in this book.

❑ Select the oval tool on the tool palette and note the options available on the lower half of the tool palette.

FIRST ANIMATION PROJECT

THE TOOL PALETTE

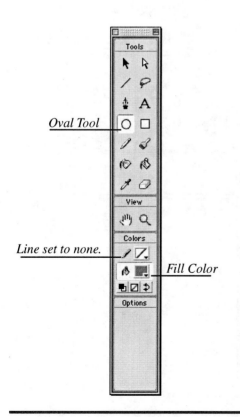

Oval Tool

Line set to none.

Fill Color

❑ Set the line ✏ to none ☑ (no line) and the
fill 🪣 to red.

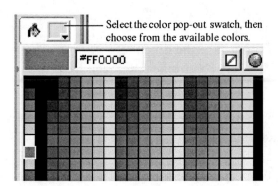

Select the color pop-out swatch, then
choose from the available colors.

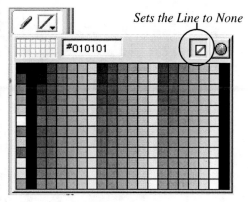

Sets the Line to None

Line color set to none

DRAWING ON THE STAGE

❑ Draw a circle on the Center of the stage.

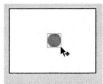

To draw with the oval tool click and drag diagonally.

❑ Click on frame 2 of the timeline .

INSERTING KEYFRAMES

❑ Select the Insert-Keyframe command from the
menu bar to insert a new keyframe.

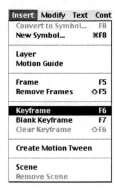

Insert	Modify	Text	Cont
Convert to Symbol...			F8
New Symbol...			⌘F8
Layer			
Motion Guide			
Frame			F5
Remove Frames			⇧F5
Keyframe			F6
Blank Keyframe			F7
Clear Keyframe			⇧F6
Create Motion Tween			
Scene			
Remove Scene			

❑ Select the pointer tool from the tool palette
and drag the circle a little to the right.

CREATING MOVEMENT

❑ Click on frame 3 of the timeline

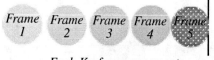

Each Keyframe represents
one frame of the animation.

PLAYING THE ANIMATION

Control	Window	Help
Play		Return
Rewind		⌥⌘R
Step Forward		.
Step Backward		,
Test Movie		⌘Enter
Debug Movie		⇧⌘Enter
Test Scene		⌥⌘Enter
Loop Playback		
Play All Scenes		

TO STOP ANIMATION FROM PLAYING

❑ Select the Insert-Keyframe command from the menu bar. **Keyframe   F6**

❑ With the pointer tool [▶] still selected drag the circle a little further to the right.

❑ Click on frame 4 of the timeline
❑ Select the Insert-Keyframe command from the menu bar.

❑ With the pointer tool [▶] still selected drag the circle further to the right.

❑ Click on frame 5 of the timeline
❑ Select the Insert-Keyframe command from the menu bar.
❑ With the pointer tool still selected drag the circle to the right edge of the stage.

You have just completed your first simple animation in Flash.

Test the animation and see how it looks...

❑ Choose Control-Loop Playback.

❑ Then choose Control-Play, to see the animation in progress.
You should see the ball appear to move to the right edge then abruptly jump back to the center of the stage. Ideally we would want the ball to appear to strike the right edge of the stage then bounce back towards the center.

❑ To stop the animation from playing choose Control-Stop *(or hit the return key on your keyboard).*

❑ Retouch, or tweak, the animation to create smoother movement. *You may need to click back on each separate keyframe to reposition the ball so there is an equal amount of space and the ball moves more smoothly.*

After testing and tweaking the animation:
Continue creating the animation so the ball returns to the starting point in the center of the stage.

❑ Click on frame 6 of the timeline to select it, then insert a new keyframe. Move the ball slightly towards the left, *back to the center of the stage.*

❑ Click on frame 7 insert a new keyframe and move the ball further back towards the center.

❑ Continue this process until the ball has moved from the far right of the stage back to the center of the stage.
Now the ball moves to the far right then moves back towards the center.

Adding more interest to the animation
Using the following steps, the ball will get larger as it moves to the right

❑ Click on frame 1 to select the object at that point in the timeline.

❑ Using the pointer tool ▶, click on the ball on the stage, then click on the resize button ⬚ on the tool palette. *(See the diagram at right)*

❑ The ball object should now have resize handle bars.

❑ Drag a corner handle in, to make the ball smaller.

❑ Click on frame 2, and use the resize option ⬚ make the ball a little larger than frame 1.

❑ Continue by clicking on the keyframe, then clicking on the ball on the stage, and using the resize option make the ball a little larger in frames 3, 4, and 5.

CREATING THE BOUNCE

In the first 5 frames ball moves to the right.

In frames 6-10 it moves back to center.

RESIZING AN OBJECT OVER TIME

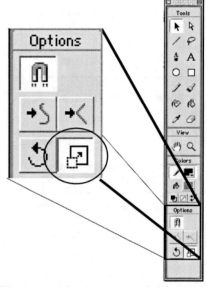

The resize Option is available on the lower half of the tool palette, when the pointer tool is selected and an object on the stage is selected.

Frame 1   Frame 2   Frame 3   Frame 4

Onion Skin

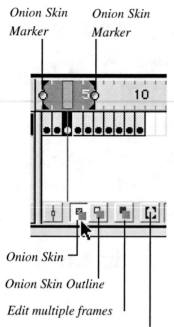

Onion Skin Marker   Onion Skin Marker

Onion Skin

Onion Skin Outline

Edit multiple frames

Modify the onion skin markers

Modify Onion Skin Markers

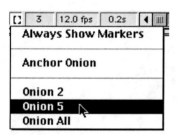

Onion Skin Outline

The ball should gradually get larger as it moves towards the right.

By now you are most likely saying I wish there was some way I could see where the ball was in the previous frame in order to know where to position it or how big to make it in the next frame"

Using the onion skinning feature:

❏ Click on frame 3 on the timeline.

❏ At the bottom of the timeline window there are three different onion skin options.

Select the first option as shown.

NOTE: With onion skinning turned on you can see several other frames which are shown lighter then the current frame.

❏ Select the modify onion skin markers button to change the settings. By default Flash uses onion 2, which shows the two frames before and after the selected frame. Change the setting to onion 5 to see the results.

❏ You can also grab and drag the onion skin marker handles to control which frames you are seeing.

❏ Try the onion skin outline button. This is a nice feature because you can clearly see which is the active frame.

❏ To turn onion skinning off click the button again. They toggle like an on/off switches.

❏ Finally the last onion skin option to try is Edit Multiple Frames. Using this option you can edit the ball on several frames at once without clicking through individual frames on the timeline. This is a great time saving feature when working with frame by frame animation

In the next three steps we'll use the onion skin feature to touch up the growing ball animation.

❑ Click on frame 3, choose the Edit Multiple Frames button, then select the Modify Markers button and set it to onion 2.

❑ With the pointer tool, click on any one of the balls, (make sure <u>only one</u> ball is selected) then select the resize button 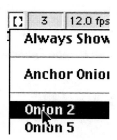 from the tool palette.

❑ Resize and reposition each ball until you are happy with the size and placement.

To finish the animation we want the ball to shrink as it moves back towards the center.

❑ Use onion skinning to assist with placement and repeat the steps from the previous pages (Resizing an object over time) to make the ball shrink as it returns to center.

❑ Turn onion skinning off, then choose Control-Play to test the movie.

A part of what makes animation fun and more interesting is exaggeration. In the real world a ball would flatten slightly when it strikes a surface. In the world of animation we want to exaggerate the impact.
If you have ever seen the road runner cartoon, when poor Wile E Coyote realizes he is about to blown up, his eyes become 3x's larger, and pop out of his head. When he falls off of a cliff and hits the ground he sinks 3 feet into the earth. We intellectually know this is not real, but because it is animation it becomes more interesting. When the anvil falls and hits Wile E. in the head, if you watch this in slow motion, his entire body is almost flattened, and expanded sideways to emphasize the impact, and then of course he gets a bump on his head that rises two feet in the air. If we wanted a realistic image of a ball striking a surface we might grab the camcorder and film it. With animation we want to emphasize the unreal quality. In a

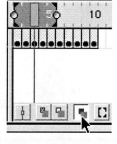

Edit multiple Frames

Modify Markers, set to 2 frames.

EXAGGERATION ADDS INTEREST

CREATING THE ILLUSION OF IMPACT.

Ball flattens on impact

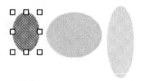

Ball wobble back to its normal shape

FURTHER EXPLORATION

WOW! we have just covered a huge amount of information, and if you are new to Flash you definitely need a break!

Take a few minutes to rest your mind. When you come back, before continuing on, take a moment to review this chapter (just skim it). These are the basics of working with Flash. Creating objects, using the timeline, and adding keyframes, onion skinning to view object placement, testing playback and making revisions, resizing and exaggerating objects to create interesting animated effects.

After you have had a chance to review the chapter try one of the "Further Exploration" projects, to see if you are comfortable with the information that has just been covered.

way animation is the ideal medium for surrealism (beyond realism).

In this next step we will exaggerate how the ball would look when it strikes a surface.

❑ Select the frame where the ball appears to strike the right edge of the stage (frame 5).

❑ Click on the ball on the stage then select the resize button from the tool palette.

❑ Stretch the ball so it appears to flatten when it strikes the side of the stage. See diagram.

❑ After the ball strikes the side of the stage and flattens it would most likely wobble. In frame 6 make the ball shorter and wider. Then in frame 7 give it less exaggerated flatten effect. *See the diagram.*

❑ Test the animation to see if the effect works.

❑ **Save this project** as "ball bounce" we will be using it in the next chapter.

Further Exploration:

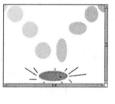

1. Create an animation where a ball drops in from the upper left corner and bounces out in the upper right.
Use onion skinning to help with placement. Use exaggeration to make it look like the ball hits the surface hard.

2. Create a 10 frame animation with a single line that appears to twirl. To make this effect work use the rotation tool.

In each frame rotate the line a little further than the previous frame. Use onion skinning to help with rotation placement.

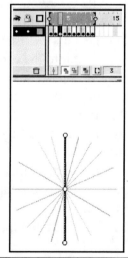

CHAPTER 3

Flash Palettes

This project is a continuation of the ball bounce you created in the previous chapter. After completing this project you should be familiar with the basic interface of Flash and ready to dive into more exciting animations.

❑ Launch Flash if it is not already running.

❑ Open the ballBounce movie created in the previous chapter.

❑ Choose Window-Panel Sets-Default Layout to rearrange the palettes.

| Panel Sets | ▶ | Default Layout |

In the upper right corner of your monitor you will see the Info palette. The Info palette provides information about the size of the selected object and it's X & Y location on the stage. As you click from frame to frame in the animation the Info should change.

❑ Click on frame 5 of the ballBounce animation. This is the frame where the ball strikes the surface.

❑ Increase the height using the Info palette. Type a larger number into the H: field then hit the tab key to apply the change.

❑ Change the location of the object on the stage using the Y: coordinate. Increase the number to move the ball down, or decrease the number to move the ball up.

Topics

Info Palette 19
Transform Palette 20
Stroke Palette 20
Fill Palette 20
Changing Gradient Settings 21
Applying a Gradient with the
Paint Bucket 21
Further Exploration 22
Importing Photoshop Images
into Flash 22

INFO PALETTE

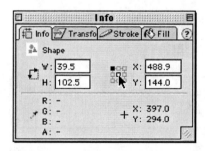

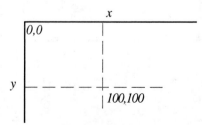

On computers, the upper left corner is the zero point of the x and y axis. Moving to the right increases the x value, and moving down increases the y value.

Transform Palette

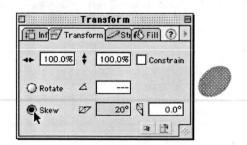

The second tab in this palette is Transform. Note that you can resize, rotate, and skew an object with the Transform palette.

❑ Click on frame 1, click on the skew button, then apply a 20° skew to the ball (type in 20 and hit the tab key on the keyboard). Note that it gives the ball the appearance of moving in a direction.

❑ Click on frames 2-4 applying a 20° skew to the ball on the stage to give it the appearance of speeding towards the right.

Stroke Palette

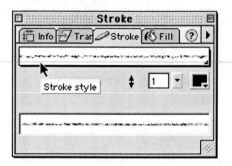

❑ The third tab is the Stroke palette. Because we did not apply a line to the ball the stroke function will have no impact.

❑ Take a moment and look through the various stroke styles, thicknesses, and color options. Flash provides some cool line styles that you may want to use later on.

❑ Select frame 6 on the timeline.

The fourth tab on this palette allows us to change fill options. Selecting the ball on the stage and changing the parameters will change the appearance of the ball.

Fill Palette

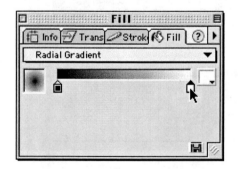

❑ Look at some of the options available on the Fill palette. Note: the object must be selected for these setting to take effect. The setup shown is an example of the radial gradient.

❑ With frame 6 selected, choose the radial gradient option from the Fill palette.

❑ Click on the white drag slider shown on the diagram. Drag it to the left to see the impact.

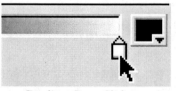

Gradient Drag Slider

❑ Note that when a drag slider is selected a color selector pop-out button appears.

Color Selector pop-out.

❑ Click on the color selector pop-out button and change the white slider of the gradient to black.

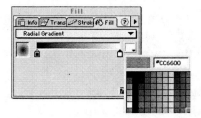

❑ Now click on the left gradient slider, then click on the pop-out color picker button and set its color to white.

❑ Now you have a black ball with a white highlight center. Hit the save button on the Fill palette in order to keep this setting available for future use. Most 3D objects don't have a highlight dead center, but Flash allows you to change this.

❑ Select the paint bucket tool 🪣 from the tool palette.

❑ With the paint bucket selected click on the ball on the stage. Note that the highlight appears wherever you click on the object. Nice feature!

❑ Work from frame 6-10 to add the gradient to the ball. Since you saved the gradient, it should be the default but can also be retrieved by clicking on the fill pop-out color selector 🪣 on the tool palette. The saved gradient is at the bottom of the color swatches.

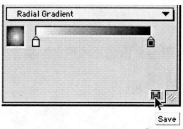

APPLYING A GRADIENT WITH THE PAINT BUCKET

Saved gradient

FYI: Extensive use of gradient fills will consume more file space and take longer to download. In the next chapter we will explore the use of symbols to reduce file size and speed download time.

Before you move on to the next chapter, take some time to explore the concepts covered.

Further Exploration:

1. Use the gradient tool in a new animation where a ball appears to roll across the stage. To create the illusion of rolling, move the highlight in each frame to make it appear to move around the object as it rolls. (I know that the highlight would not normally move, but it will create the illusion of rolling.)

2. If you completed 1 above, try adding a shadow beneath the ball object. This is actually fairly difficult with a single layer animation. When we explore layers you will find an easier solution.

3. Import a JPEG, GIF or PNG image of a head and have it bounce up and down.

A scanned image must be saved in either the, JPEG, GIF, or PNG, file format before importing. Flash prefers the PNG format.

For more information on using Photoshop, and importing scanned bitmapped images into Flash, see chapter 30.

Further Exploration

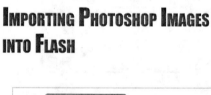

Importing Photoshop Images into Flash

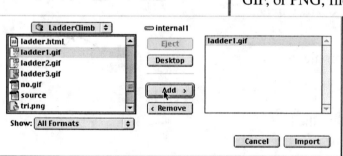

4. See if you can create an animation of two balls, each starting from a different side of the stage, that move toward the center, hit each other and bounce back towards the outer edge.

Symbols & Tweening CHAPTER 4

Two features that save time and make the animation process easier are the use of symbols and being able to tween from one keyframe to the next.

Symbols:

One of the reasons that Flash has become popular is the use of symbols. They make the creation process easier, but more importantly they dramatically reduce the final file size. Smaller file size means a shorter download time for the customers browser. Creating a symbol is easy and will be covered in the short tutorial that follows. A symbol can be used 100 times in the animation but when the final product is distributed on the web, the Flash plug-in only needs to download the original symbol once.

Tweening:

Tweening is common in most sophisticated anima-tion applications. Historically when producing something like an animated cartoon, the primary artist would produce the key frames of the anima-tion. For a ten second animation there might be twenty or more key frames that would capture the most critical points of the animation. Then an aspiring animation artists, or "Tweener", would produce the frames in-between the key frames. Computer tweening is by no means as sophisticated as an aspiring animation artist. It will not take two pictures of a person who is walking, and change leg, arm and head position to create the in-between frames. On the other hand, if you have a ball sym-bol on the left side of the stage, then insert a keyframe ten frames later with the ball symbol on the right side of the stage, Flash can generate the transition frames in-between. This is only one example as you will see in the chapters that follow.

Lets begin!!

Topics

CREATING A GRAPHIC SYMBOL 24
LIBRARY PALETTE 25
SYMBOL EDITOR 25
ANIMATION VANISHED? 25
TWEENING 26
THE FRAME PALETTE 26
FADING OVER TIME...................... 27
SAVE EVERYTHING 27
EXPERIMENTING WITH TWEENING ... 27
REVIEW QUESTIONS 28
ADDITIONAL EXPLORATION 28

CREATING A GRAPHIC SYMBOL

❑ Launch Flash.

❑ Choose Window-Panel Sets-Default Layout to rearrange the palettes.

❑ Create a ball object on the stage.

❑ Click on frame 1 in the timeline to select the ball.
Clicking on the key frame will select both the fill and the line for the ball.

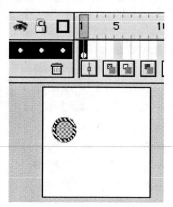

❑ With the ball object selected choose
Insert-Convert To Symbol...

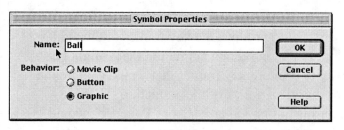

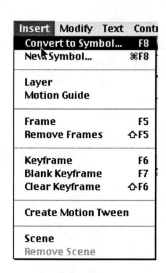

❑ Enter a name for the symbol and choose the graphic button, then hit OK.
Later chapters will cover the button and movie clip symbols. Once a graphic is converted into a symbol its appearance, on the stage, changes. It is contained in a light blue box and also has a center point.

❑ Delete the ball from the stage.
Converting an object into a graphic symbol also places a copy of the symbol in the Flash library.

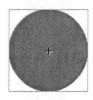

❑ Select the Window-Library menu, to display the library palette and to view the symbol.

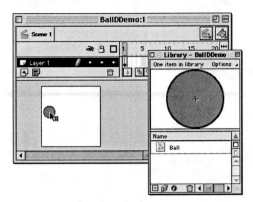

About the symbol editor: Because the ball is now saved as a symbol it cannot be edited on the stage. To edit the ball you would need to open it in the symbol editor.

To enter the symbol editor double click on the graphic symbol in the library or double click on the ball on the stage. You can tell you are in the symbol editor by looking at the upper left corner, of the main window, above the Timeline.

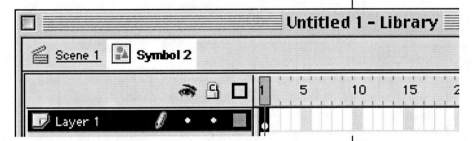

To exit the symbol editor, click on the Scene1 button. This will take you out of the symbol editor and back to the animation stage.

Important: If you are working in Flash and it appears that your animation has vanished, look above the time line to see if you accidentally entered the symbol editor. It is one of those things that can be disconcerting while you are first learning Flash but will become second nature as you grow more comfortable with this application.

To exit the symbol editor click on the Scene button.

TWEENING

When tweening in Flash the timeline must have two Keyframes. Flash then generates the frames in-between based on the characteristics of the object in the first and second Keyframe

Tweening: Flash will generate the transition frames in-between two **keyframes**.

❑ Select frame 1 on the timeline and drag the "Ball" graphic symbol from the Library palette onto the left edge of the stage.

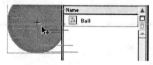

❑ Once the graphic is in place on the stage, click on frame 10 in the timeline.

❑ Choose Insert-Keyframe, to insert a new keyframe at frame 10, see diagram.

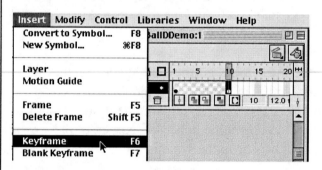

❑ With frame 10 still selected drag the ball (which is on the stage) to the right edge of the stage.

❑ Click on keyframe 1 and you'll note that the ball remains on the left edge of the stage.

THE FRAME PALETTE

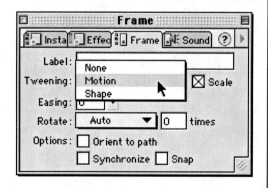

If you see a dotted line between the keyframes (no arrow) on your motion tween it means there is a problem. On common reason is that the tweened object (on the stage) is not a actually a symbol.

❑ With frame 1 highlighted, select the **Frame** palette in the lower right corner of your monitor.

❑ Select the tweening pop-out menu and select Motion.

❑ After tweening has been turned on, you should now see an arrow between keyframe 1 and 10 on the timeline.

❑ Select Control-Play to test the animation.

Adding effects to the tween

❏ Click once on frame 10 in the Timeline.

❏ Select the Effect tab from the palette in the lower right corner of your monitor.

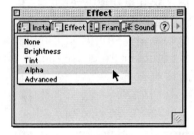

Look at some of the different option that are available as effects. Brightness of course allows you to change the brightness or darkness of the image, Tint allow you to play with the selected objects Hue or color, Alpha allows transparency changes, and advanced allows you to play with both color and transparency.

❏ Choose the Alpha Effect and set the Alpha to 0. This will make the object invisible.
Because this object is visible on frame 1 and has a "tween" it will fade over the course of the animation.

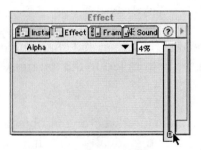

❏ Play the Animation again.
Remember you can loop the animation by selecting the command from the Control menu.

❏ Experiment with some of the other effects options, size, and rotation before closing this project.

FADING OVER TIME

SAVE EVERYTHING

Additional Exploration

SAVE EVERYTHING!! Anything you create or produce in Flash should be saved, no matter how simple. Later we will discuss how you can re-use symbols and animations.

A simple ball moving from left to right may not seem like much now, but later, when saved as a movie clip, and combined with animated type and images it may add an element of interest and be exactly what you are looking for. I frequently find that simple experimental animations are exactly what I need to compliment a complex project. Rather than recreate that simple animation over from scratch it is quicker to re-use pieces from previous works.

Additional Exploration: See if you can create the following

❑ Create a new graphic symbol.
If you are successful it should appear in your library palette.

❑ Create a tweened animation where the object remains static but fades in and out over time.

❑ Create a tweened animation where type rotates while it moves across the stage.

❑ Create type rotating, fading in and changing color as it moves from the bottom left to the top right of the stage.

❑ Create a simple animation where your object starts out as invisible and gradually fades in as it moves from top to bottom.

❑ Create a new animation where your object moves from lower right to upper left and changes color along the way.

Review Questions

Why are symbols so important in Flash?

How can a graphic be added to the library palette?

What is tweening?

How can you access and exit the symbol editor?

How can you create tweening between two keyframes?

How do you know if you are in the symbol editor?

If the timeline displays an arrow between two keyframes what does it mean?

How can the color effects of an instance of a symbol be changed?

How would you make a graphic appear to fade out over time?

How would you make a graphic change color over time?

You are going to absolutely fall in love with this feature! It is so cool!

This short 2-page project explores the shape tween with very simple objects, the next project explores the shape tween using text. This is a very limited exploration of what can be done with shape tweening so I encourage you to explore further on your own. This is an effect that one could easily get lost in and spend hours exploring.

The previous chapter demonstrated a motion tween. The motion tween requires that the object first be converted into a symbol. On the other hand, shape tweens only work with vector graphics that have not been converted into symbols, as you will see in this short demo.

Topics

SHAPE TWEEN 29
PENCIL TOOL OPTIONS 30
WHAT IS A BLANK KEYFRAME? 30
KEYFRAME SHORTCUTS 30
TWEEN/FRAME PALETTE 31
SHAPE VS. MOTION TWEEN........... 32

SHAPE TWEEN

PENCIL TOOL OPTIONS

WHAT IS A BLANK KEYFRAME?

*A regular keyframe copies the graphics from the previous keyframe. A **blank keyframe** does **not** copy the information and allows you to start with a new graphic.*

KEYFRAME SHORTCUTS

❑ Launch Flash and create a new document.

❑ Choose Modify-Movie and set the background to black.

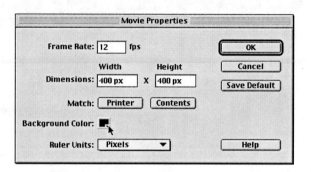

❑ Select the pencil tool and choose bright green as the line color and smooth as the pencil option, as shown in the diagram.

❑ Draw a simple object in the upper left corner of the stage, such as the example shown below.

Remember that you can change the line thickness using the Stroke palette.

❑ Click on frame 20 of the timeline then insert a **blank** keyframe at frame 20.

Timeline keyboard shortcuts:
F6 adds a normal keyframe and the
F7 adds a blank keyframe.
***Control-click** on the timeline with the Mac or*
***Right-click** on the timeline with the PC,*
to display a menu of timeline options.

❑ With frame 20 selected (in the timeline) draw an unfilled circle in the lower right corner of the stage.

Turn the fill option off and change the line color and thickness for the circle using the Stroke and Fill palettes.

❑ Select frame 1 in the timeline.

❑ Select the Frame palette (it should be in the lower right corner on your monitor) and set Tweening to shape.

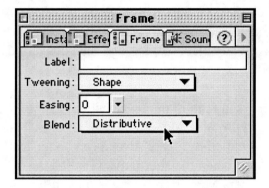

❑ Choose Control-Play to test the animation.

❑ Try changing the shape tween to angular and test again.

| Blend : | Distributive |
| | Angular |

❑ Experiment with the easing in/out options to see the effects.

Note: Because the graphics are NOT symbols they will accept a shape tween. If you tried a motion tween, with these same objects, you would see an exclamation symbol on the palette which warns that the effect will not work.

TWEEN/FRAME PALETTE

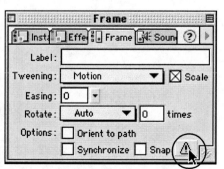

Tween warning information

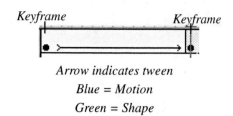

Keyframe   Keyframe

Arrow indicates tween
Blue = Motion
Green = Shape

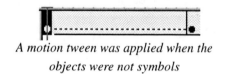

A motion tween was applied when the objects were not symbols

SHAPE VS. MOTION TWEEN

Frame 1   Frame 15

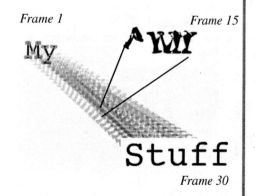

Stuff

Frame 30

Some tips about Tweening:

Flash provides different visual information, on the timeline, based on the type of tween that you use. A motion tween is displayed as blue with an arrow and a shape tween displays as green.

Tweens only work from keyframe to keyframe. The idea behind tweens is to produce frames IN-BE-TWEEN 2 keyframes. If you ever attempt to create a tween and see a dashed line instead of an arrow the problem lies in either the beginning or ending keyframe. Motion tweening will only work if the object is a symbol whereas shape tweening will only work if the object is not a symbol. Attempting to shape tween two symbols will produce a dashed line indicating the tween will not work. Attempting to motion tween an abject that has not been converted to a symbol will not work.

The shape tween feature in Flash is definitely very cool, and can produce some interesting effects. The fact that it is called a "Shape" tween can be misleading, especially when the alternative is called the "Motion" tween. Motion tweening is most often used when you need a controlled change from keyframe to keyframe. If you are changing the objects position, size, rotation, or color you should use the motion tween, even if the object is not moving. Shape tween produces very organic but unpredictable in-between frames. As an artist or designer this may be exactly what you are looking for, but if you need transformations with predictable results then motion tweening is a better choice.

The diagram at the left shows the word "My" tweening into the word "Stuff" (over a 30 frame shape tween). When viewed as an onion skin it appears to be a logical transformation. But when one looks at the individual frames (such as frame 15) the transformation is visually interesting but also something that one would not predict.

CHAPTER 6

Melting Type Animation

Topics

SHAPE TWEENED TYPE 33
SETUP 33
THE CHARACTER PALETTE 34
TURNING TEXT INTO A GRAPHIC 35
TYPE TWEENING TIPS 36

SHAPE TWEENED TYPE

Shape Tweening with type is easy and can produce some visually powerful results. When Flash produces type it is not a graphic symbol, but it is not a raw vector shape either. To perform a shape tween the text must be converted into a raw vector shape. So, to use type in a shape tween, it must be "broken apart".

SETUP

❏ Create a new Flash document with a background color of white, size is not critical.

❏ Choose Window-Panel Sets-Default Layout to reset the palettes.

| Panel Sets ▶ | Default Layout |

❏ Select the text tool A from the tool palette.

❑ Select the Character palette to select a font, size and color.

❑ Click on the stage to set the insertion point and type in your name.

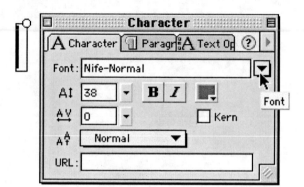

❑ Select frame 30 on the timeline and insert a **blank keyframe**.

Remember you can Option-Click (Mac) or Right-Click (PC) or use the F7 key to insert the Blank Keyframe.

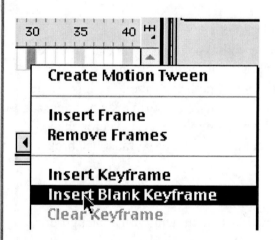

❑ With frame 30 selected, choose the Character palette and change the font and size.

❑ In the lower right corner of the stage **type in the word "Flash"**.

If you tried to perform a shape tween at this point the type would vanish after frame 1 and the new type would appear on frame 30. In order for Flash to produce a shape tween you will need to break the text apart, which is easy to do.

❑ With frame 30 selected choose
Modify-Break Apart. *(See diagram)*
This converts the type into an vector graphic.

❑ Select frame 1 and again choose Modify-Break Apart.

Flash can now perform a shape tween between the two vector graphics.

❑ With frame 1 still selected choose the Frame palette and set the tween to shape.

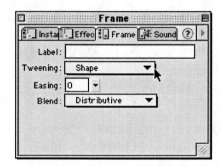

❑ Test the movie using Control-Play.
Some of the effects that the type goes through along the way can be pretty amazing.

TYPE TWEENING TIPS

Shape tweening with type.

This is a cool effect and I'm sure you can think of a variety of ways to use this effect in your web pages.

It is important that the type is "Broken Apart" before applying the shape tween. Sometimes the type will vanish after the first keyframe then reappear at the last keyframe. I do not know exactly why this happens, but here are a couple of suggestions that should help to resolve this problem.

If you are changing the color of the type from the first to the second keyframe and the type vanishes or the tween is not as exciting as you would like try one of the following.

1. Create the type in keyframe 1, then create the type in keyframe 2 using the same color. Break the type apart so it is in vector graphic format. After it has been broken apart use the pointer tool to select the type in keyframe 2, then use the Fill palette to change the color. For some reason, I get much better shape tweens using this procedure.

2. Shape tweening appears to work better with lines than with objects. I do not know exactly why this is but if we looked at the computer algorithm that produces the shape tween, I'm sure we would find the answer. Sometimes the shape tween is not very interesting. Because shape tweening works better with lines the following tip cab be used to change or enhance the effect. Select the first keyframe, then select the pencil tool and set it to the same color as the type. Draw lines inside the type on keyframe 1. Keep the lines inside the type in order to avoid distorting the type. Select the ending keyframe, and with the pencil tool set to the same color as the type in the ending keyframe, draw lines inside the type. If you replay the shape tween you should now see much more interesting transition.

Solar Explosion

CHAPTER 7

Topics

SETUP 37
MOTION TWEEN 37
SETTING THE LINE TO NONE 38
CHANGING GRADIENT SETTINGS 38
CREATING A GRAPHIC SYMBOL 39
RESIZING A GRAPHIC 40
CREATING THE EXPLOSION 40
RESIZING THE STAGE 41
LARGER THAN THE STAGE 41
CREATING A MOTION TWEEN 42
RESIZING THE MOVIE 43
CLOSING THE TEST MOVIE 43
TESTING THE MOVIE. 43
SPECIAL EFFECTS WITH SKEWING ... 43
CHANGING ANIMATION SPEED 44

This project is a blast!!
The goal is to create a solar explosion. Turns out this effect is very simple to create and also downloads very fast on the web, because it requires only one graphic symbol. While it downloads fast, it does not play as fast as I would like because we are asking Flash to perform some major changes over a few short frames.

❑ Launch Flash and create a new document.

❑ Choose Modify-Movie and set the background to black.

❑ Choose Window-Panel Sets-Default Layout to reset the palettes.

SETUP

Panel Sets	▶	Default Layout

❏ Select the oval tool on the tool palette

❏ On the tool palette set the stroke to none.

SETTING THE LINE TO NONE

❏ Select the Fill palette and set the fill type to radial gradient.
By default my gradient settings come up with the inner part of the gradient as black and the outer edge as white, we want to reverse this.

CHANGING GRADIENT SETTINGS

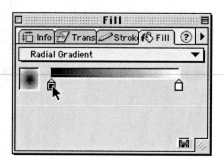

❏ Click on the black gradient tab then choose

the color pop-out (on the fill palette) to change

this color to white.

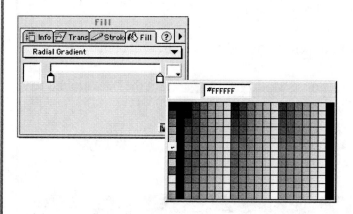

❏ Click on the right gradient tab and set the color to black.

❏ The radial gradient tab should now look like the following...

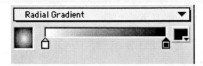

❏ Draw a circle on the stage.

❏ Click on frame 1 of the timeline to select the object. *The object may appear distorted when selected, but do not fear, this is the way that Flash lets you know the object is selected.*

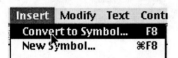

❏ Choose Insert-Convert to Symbol.

Insert	Modify	Text	Conti
Convert to Symbol...			F8
New Symbol...			⌘F8

CREATING A GRAPHIC SYMBOL

❏ Make sure to select the graphic button and name this symbol. Call it "Sun".

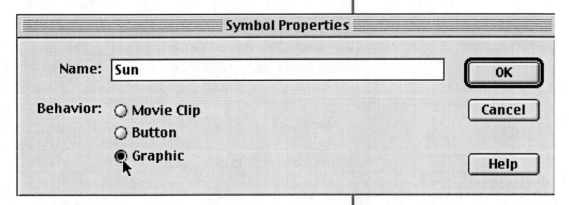

❏ Insert a keyframe at frame 20.

❏ Click on frame 1 in the timeline.

❏ Select the pointer tool ![pointer] from the tool palette.

❏ Select the resize option from the tool palette.

RESIZING A GRAPHIC

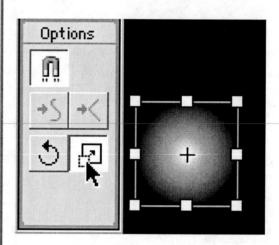

At the beginning of the animation we want the sun to appear as a small dot.

❏ Use the resize handles to make the sun object small.

On frame 20 we can leave the object as is. The idea is that from frame 1-20 the sun will slowly grow in size then explode quickly from frame 20-35.

Creating the Explosion

CREATING THE EXPLOSION

❏ Insert a keyframe at frame 35.

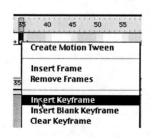

In the lower left corner of the stage there is a pop-out menu that allows you zoom-in or zoom-out on the size of the stage.

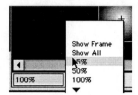

❑ Set the stage size to 25%.

❑ With frame 35 still selected, click on the resize button on the tool palette, and increase the size of the sun until it completely covers the stage (or larger).

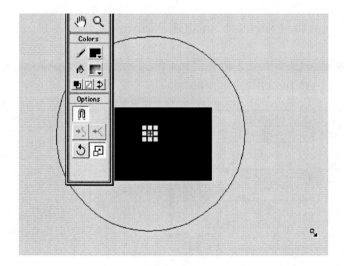

❑ With the resize option still selected stretch the width. (Make the object wider.)

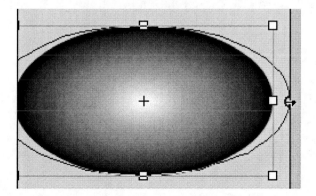

MAKING AN OBJECT GROW
LARGER THAN THE STAGE

❑ Insert a keyframe at frame 60.

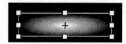

❑ Select the resize button 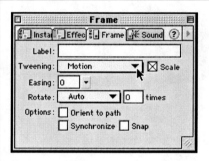 from the tool palette and make the sun small again, but leave it somewhat wide.

Adding the tweens to finish the effect.

❑ Click on frame 1 and select the Frame palette.
❑ Set the tweening to motion.

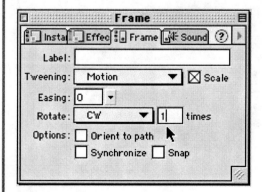

❑ Click on frame 20 and set the tweening to motion.

❑ Click on frame 35, set the tweening to motion and include a clockwise rotation of 1 times.

CREATING A MOTION TWEEN

❑ Choose Control-Test Movie to have this movie display in it's own separate window.

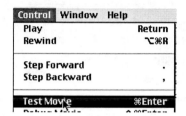

❑ Resize the movie window so it covers your entire monitor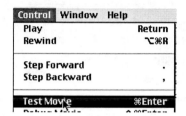

❑ To exit the movie player, after viewing the movie, click the close [button] button.

Adding a twist to the explosion

❑ Select frame 35 on the timeline, turn off the rotation option on the Frame palette (by setting rotation to none) then, select the Transform palette, and turn on the skew option and apply a 20° skew.

❑ Most likely the sun will shrink on the stage, so select the resize tool and drag it back out until it covers well beyond the edges of the stage. Make it as big as possible.

❑ Choose Control-Test Movie and make the movie window larger so it covers your entire monitor. The skew creates some interesting effects!

❑ See if you can add frames to the end of this animation so the sun object appears to slowly shrink back down into a tiny spot of light before it loops back into the explosion.

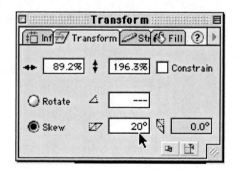

CHANGING ANIMATION SPEED

To make something appear to happen quickly use less frames for the transition but expect the transition to be more jerky. To make something appear to happen slowly use more frames for the transition and the transition will appear smoother. To have the sun shrink slowly you may want to add a new keyframe out at frame 130 or greater.

As long as we are discussing animation speed this is a good time to discuss Frame Rate, "frames per second".

Frame Rate: 12 **fps**

Under the Modify Menu-Movie Properties you can "adjust" the frame rate. This is a global setting that effects the entire movie, (unlike applications like Director where you can set the frame rate to different speeds at different parts of the movie). You might assume that setting the frame rate to high number will guarantee faster playback but unfortunately this is not the case. A simple animation with a shape tween, will slow your frame rate to 12 fps or even lower depending upon the complexity of the tween.

How can I get rid of the "jerky" playback?
The jerky appearance that you notice is more often than not attributed to something I refer to as proximity. As an artist, you are working closely with your project and will likely watch it many times. As a result you will notice minor imperfections that the casual user will not. It is helpful to remember that the casual web observer will see your 10 second animation for 10 seconds. Another internet reality to consider is that the user with the newer faster computer may experience a better animation than the user with an older slower computer. With some animations it might be possible to smooth out the animation by experimenting with Motion Trails (as discussed in chapter 28).

CHAPTER 8

The spinning text project works with a motion tween. The interesting thing about type is that it does not need to be converted into a symbol in order to apply a motion tween. While it does not appear in the library, Flash recognizes it as an object.

❑ Create a new Flash document with a background color of black, size is not critical.

❑ Choose Window-Panel Sets-Default Layout to reset the palettes.

❑ Select the text tool A from the tool palette.

SETUP

CHARACTER ATTRIBUTES

❏ Select the Character palette to choose a font, size and color (bright green is a good choice).

❏ Click on the stage to set the insertion point and type in your name.

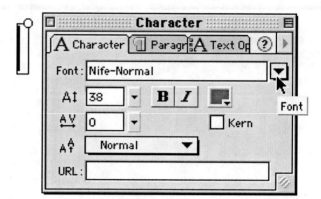

❏ Select frame 30 on the timeline and insert a keyframe.

Insert Keyframe

❏ Select frame 1 on the timeline.

MOTION TWEEN

❏ Select the pointer tool ➤ , and choose the resize button on the tool palette to make the type smaller.

❏ In the Frame palette set the tween to motion, and rotation to CW (clockwise) 1 time.

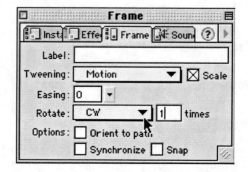

❏ Choose Control-Play to test the movie.

❏ After testing the movie, click on frame 1 and experiment with the easing options on the Frame palette.

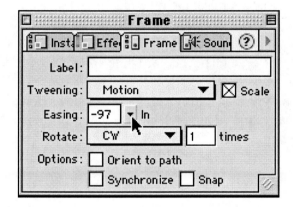

❏ With Frame 1 selected choose Modify-Transform-Edit Center. See diagram.

❏ This will produce a crosshair symbol in the center of your graphic. Select the crosshair and drag it to the left as shown below.

❏ Replay the movie to see the effect.

❏ You can also modify the center point of the image in the final keyframe to add even more interesting effects.

CHANGING AN OBJECTS CENTER POINT

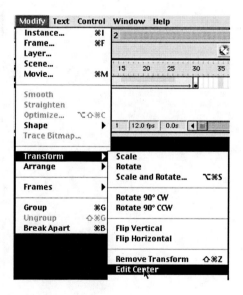

Additional Exploration

• See if you can have the type animate across the stage while spinning.

• Try to make the type grow larger while spinning then shrink back down .

• See if you can make the type fade in, while spinning.

• Make the type change color while spinning.

• Create type that spins clockwise then slows down, and finally spins counterclockwise while shrinking and fading.

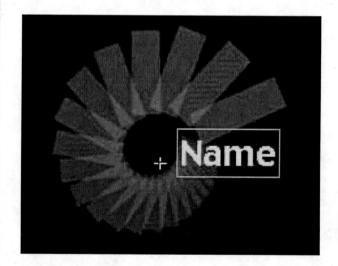

CHAPTER 9

Fun With Flash Layers

Since many Flash users are familiar with Photoshop the concept of layers becomes fairly easy to grasp. On the other hand if you are not familiar with Photoshop, you will gain skills using Flash, that will help you as you begin to explore other applications.

Flash uses layers in several different ways.
1. It is a way to help organize the parts of your animation into logical pieces.
2. It is a way to help position one object in front of another.
3. It is required to create multiple tweens in an animation.
4. It is a way to determine which parts of your movie will be streamed to a customers first, ie should they get the bottom layer first while the other layers download or should they get the top layer first.

Topics

FLASH LAYERS 49
PROJECT SETUP - REVIEW 50
ADDING NEW LAYERS 51
NAMING LAYERS 51
HIDING A LAYER 51
LOCKING A LAYER 51
SECOND ANIMATION -NEW LAYER .. 51
SEPARATE ANIMATION ON LAYER 2 52
PROBLEMS ? : SYMBOL EDITOR ... 52
MOTION TWEEN ON LAYER 2 53
UNLOCKING A LAYER 53
FURTHER EXPLORATION: 54

FLASH LAYERS

Layers allow you to add in additional timelines.

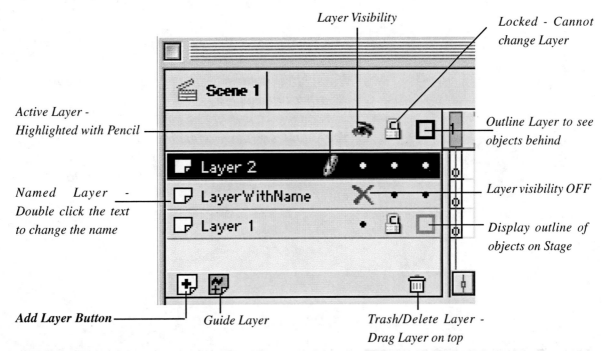

Layer Visibility

Locked - Cannot change Layer

Active Layer - Highlighted with Pencil

Outline Layer to see objects behind

Named Layer - Double click the text to change the name

Layer visibility OFF

Display outline of objects on Stage

Add Layer Button

Guide Layer

Trash/Delete Layer - Drag Layer on top

PROJECT
SETUP - REVIEW

By now you should be familiar with the following setup. Create a new flash movie that is 400 x 400 pixels with a grey background. A blue ball starts in the upper left corner and fades out as it moves to the lower right corner of the stage.

❑ Create a new movie

❑ Set the stage size to 400 x 400 pixels and the background color to light grey.

❑ Select the circle tool and create a simple dark blue ball with no line. Place the ball in the upper left corner of the stage.
If you have problems with the above steps refer back to chapters 2 and 3.

❑ Convert your ball into a graphic symbol.

❑ Check the symbol library to make sure the ball exists as a symbol.

❑ Click on frame 20 of the timeline and add a new keyframe.

❑ With frame 20 selected move the ball to the lower right corner of the stage.

❑ Set the ball so it is transparent in frame 20.

❑ Create a motion tween between frame 1 and 20.

If you have problems with the previous six steps refer back to chapter 4.

You should now have a one layer animation that is 20 frames long where the ball symbol starts in the upper left corner and fades out as it moves to the lower right.

❑ Double click on the label of layer 1, until it becomes highlighted. Change the name to "BallLeftToRight".

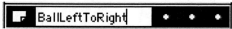

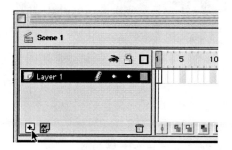

❑ Click on the plus symbol 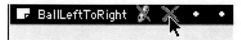 under layer 1 to add a new layer.

❑ Click on the visibility button for layer 1. *Turn off the visibility of layer 1 in order to make it easier to work with the objects we will create for layer 2.*

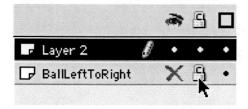

❑ Click on the locked button for layer 1 in order to insure that we do not accidently modify the animation we have created there.

❑ Click on frame 1 in Layer 2 (on the timeline) to make sure it is active.

CREATING A SEPARATE ANIMATION ON LAYER 2

SYMBOL EDITOR PROBLEMS

Note: If you accidentally double click on the ball in the library, Flash will open the symbol editor. To exit the symbol editor click in the upper left corner, above the timeline on the Scene1 icon.

Frame 1 of Layer 2

❑ Drag a copy of the ball symbol from the library to the middle of the right edge of the stage.

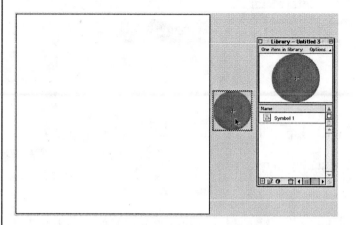

❑ Click on frame 20 of layer 2 on the timeline and add a new keyframe.

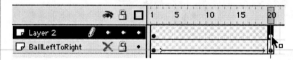

❑ With frame 20 of layer 2 selected drag the ball on layer 2 from to the far left edge of the stage.

❑ Click on frame 1 of layer 2. Select the Frame palette located in the lower right corner of your monitor.

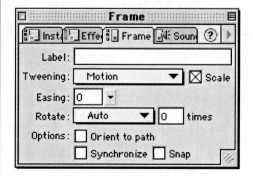

❏ Create a motion tween between frame 1 and 20 of layer 2.

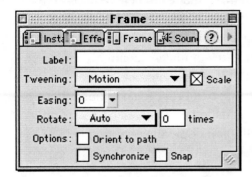

You should now have an animation on layer 2 where the ball starts at the right edge of the stage and is invisible and gradually fades in while it moves to the left edge of the stage. If not work back through the previous six steps to create the animation on layer 2.

❏ Unlock layer 1 and make it visible.

❏ Test this animation.

If all went well the ball on layer 1 fades out as it moves from left to right, while the ball on Layer 2 fades in as it moves from right to left.

MOTION TWEEN ON LAYER 2

UNLOCKING A LAYER

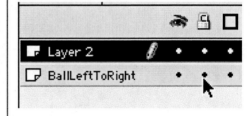

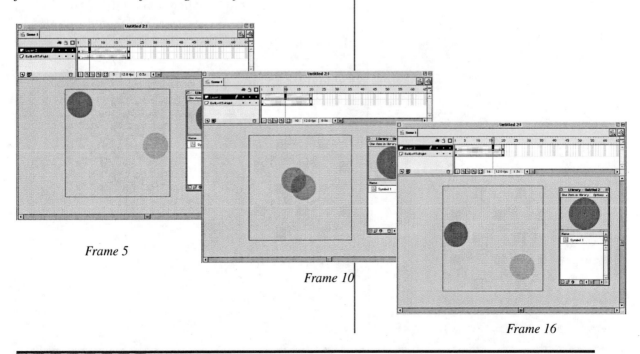

Frame 5

Frame 10

Frame 16

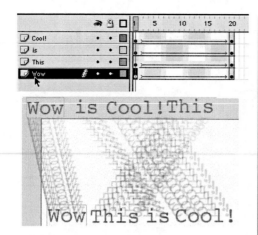

This has been a basic introduction to layer animation. While Flash is capable of tweening, it is important to remember that each layer can only contain a single tween. If you wanted multiple words to tween in from different directions, then each word needs to be animated separately and to have its own layer. If you wanted individual letters to move onto the stage in order to spell out a word then each letter needs to be animated on a separate layer. Additionally you could have motion tweens on some of the layers while shape tweens are acting on other layers.

FURTHER EXPLORATION

Further Exploration

❑ Create a new layer in which the ball moves to the center by frame 10 then changes direction at frame 10 and exits the stage. (Can you figure this one out, the answer lies in keyframes)

❑ Create a new movie. Create a ball that looks 3D using the gradient tools. Use layers to have a shadow move with the ball while it moves across the stage.

❑ Create a new movie where two words come spinning in from different directions then drop into place to make a statement.

Remember nothing goes to waste. Save everything you create. It can be recycled when we begin to explore movie clips.

A couple of students asked how to create an explosion with Flash. Since this is an interesting topic, and illustrates the concept of synchronizing animation on several layers, I've created this project to demonstrate one possible approach. Of course, with Flash, there are a wide variety of ways that explosions could be created.

Photoshop users: the concepts covered here are very similar to what you might do in Photoshop if you wanted to create a series of images representing an explosion. First you would create an object. Then you would break the object into pieces, putting each piece into a separate layer. Then you would select each piece, on the different layers, and move them apart a little at a time to create a series of images of the object breaking apart.

To keep this project from getting longer than it needs to be I'll keep the objects simple. I encourage you to walk back through this handout later and try creating something more complex. There are some suggestion for further exploration at the end of the chapter.

Topics

MOTION TWEENED EXPLOSION 55
USING THE LASSO TOOL 56
DRAGGING A SYMBOL FROM THE
LIBRARY PALETTE 57
EACH LAYER SHOULD CONTAIN 57
SYMBOL, REMAIN IN THE LIBRARY ...57
REASSEMBLE THE CIRCLE 58
KEYFRAMES ON SEVERAL LAYERS. ..58
WHAT IS AN IN-BETWEEN FRAME?..59
PROJECT SUMMARY 59
INTRODUCTION TO ACTIONSCRIPT ...60

LAYER ANIMATION
MOTION TWEENED
EXPLOSION

USING THE LASSO TOOL

❑ Create a circle object that is filled with red and has the line set to none.

❑ Select the lasso tool  and divide the circle into quarters. See example below.

❑ Use the pointer tool 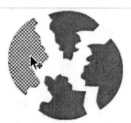 and select one chunk of the circle, as shown in the example below.

❑ With the one chunk selected choose Insert-Convert To Symbol.

❑ Name the selected graphic in a manner that helps to remember its location, such as "leftChunk".

❑ Repeat the process with the remaining three chunks of the circle. Give each chunk a name that will help you identify its location or purpose.

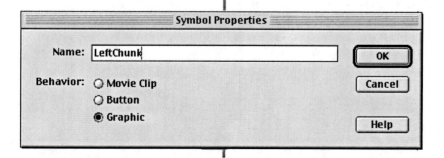

© KALDAHL

❏ After all of the pieces have been converted to symbols, select and delete all of the items on the stage. Do not delete items in the library palette.

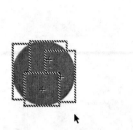

Delete objects from stage

DO NOT delete symbols from the Library

❏ Create 3 new layers on the timeline, as shown.

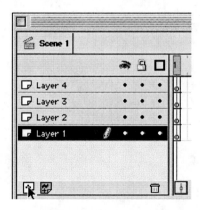

Put a separate symbol (chunk of ball) onto each separate layer as described in the following steps.

❏ **Make layer 1 active** (by clicking on frame 1 of layer 1) and drag the "left chunk" onto the stage.

❏ **Make layer 2 active** and drag the "top chunk" onto the stage.

❏ **Make layer 3 active** and drag the "right chunk" onto the stage.

❏ **Make layer 4 active** and drag the "bottom chunk" onto the stage.

WITH EACH PIECE OF THE BALL ON A SEPARATE LAYER REASSEMBLE THE CIRCLE

❏ Select the pointer tool and reassemble the circle. *You may need to use the directional keys on the keyboard to nudge the pieces into the correct position.*

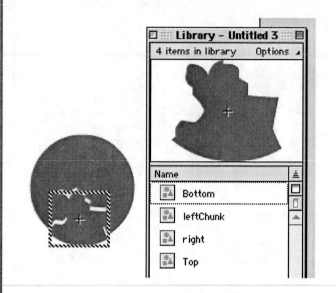

Review: The circle was broken apart, each part converted to a symbol, each symbol placed on a separate layer then the circle reassembled.

CREATING KEYFRAMES ON SEVERAL LAYERS AT ONCE.

Creating multiple keyframes.

❏ Click on frame 40 of layer 4. Hold down the SHIFT key and click on frame 40 of layer 1. *This should have the effect of selecting frame 40 for all of the layers at once.*

❏ Select Insert-Keyframe, from the menu-bar. Your timeline should now look like the example shown.

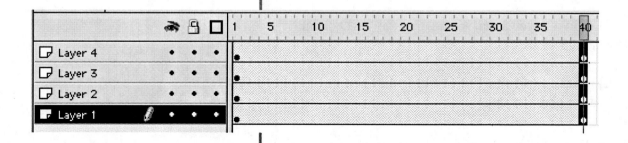

❏ Select the first frame of layer 1 and set the Frame palette to Motion Tween, as shown below

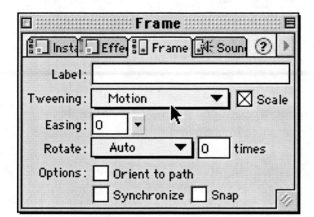

WHAT IS AN IN-BETWEEN FRAME?

In-Between Frames:
The Frames that are between
the Keyframes.

❏ Repeat the above step for the other 3 layers.

❏ Your timeline should look like the example.

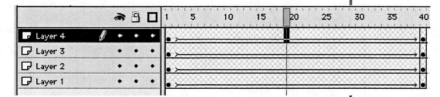

❏ With frame 40 of layer 1 selected, drag the circle chunk off the stage, in the direction that you would expect it to move if it exploded, as shown in the diagram below.

❏ Repeat the above step (In FRAME 40) for the remaining layers.

PROJECT SUMMARY

Summary:
In frame 1 the four pieces of the circle are together. In frame 40 the four pieces have been moved off the stage. The motion tween produces the in-between movement as the circle explodes and moves outward.

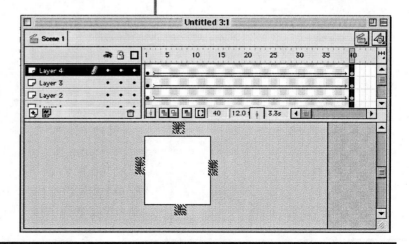

To make this effect happen more quickly you can reduce the number of frames.

To make this effect more realistic you can break the object into more pieces.

You can also add another layer, where smoke and fire burst out from the center of the explosion.

For additional effects you can have some of the pieces rotate and spin as they exit the stage.

FURTHER EXPLORATION
INTRODUCTION TO ACTIONSCRIPT

Flash allows you to place scripts in two different places. Frame actions which are scripts on the timeline, and Object Actions which are scripts applied to objects on the stage such as buttons.

❑ Save this movie.

❑ Choose Control-Test Movie to see the effect.
If all went well you should see each piece of the circle moving outward from the center.

Further Exploration:

1. Import a Photoshop Scanned image, use the lasso tool to break it apart, and repeat the steps in this project to create an explosion of the scanned image.

2. Try synchronizing the Solar Explosion with this project. Create the effect that when the solar explosion occurs the object breaks apart. To get the best results the solar explosion would occur on layer 1, and the objects will need to be on layers 2 or greater.

Notice that when you test the movie, it keeps looping. To get the movie to stop at the end use this simple ActionScript.
1. Using the stop command.
• Add a new layer to the timeline.
• Click on the last frame of the new layer and insert a keyframe.

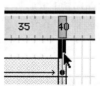

• Double click on the new keyframe to display the Frame Actions dialog box, shown below.

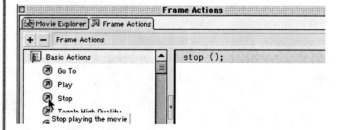

• In the Frame Actions dialog, click on the Basic Actions book to display the various basic actions.
• Double click on the Stop action. (shown above)
• Choose Control-Test Movie to see the effect.

CHAPTER 11

Publishing Flash on the Web

By now you are ready to publish your work.

This chapter discusses two options for export. The first is the Flash SWF web format and the second is the animated GIF format.

For the most part you will want to use the Flash SWF format. It insures that all of the features that you create in your Flash movie will be available on the web. In addition it provides some of the best compression available on the internet.

The second publishing option discussed, is the animated GIF format. Why export a Flash movie as an animated GIF?

The only reason that I can think of, to use an animated GIF instead of a Flash SWF file is that the GIF format does not require a special plug-in. A little bit of user friendly eye candy on the opening page of our site.

Flash does a pretty good job of squeezing the file size down for animated GIF's. If you have used animated GIF's on your web site then you know this is an important issue because compared to the Flash SWF file format, GIF files are monstrously huge. Flash can also generate an image map on your animated GIF in order to keep links in tact. Of course the problems with the animated GIF file format is that it does not support Flash interactivity, vector compression, and sound to name a few. Such is the price we pay for being user friendly.

Topics

EXPORTING & SAVING FOR THE WEB 61
PUBLISH SWF FILES FOR DISTRIBUTION ON THE WEB. 62
PUBLISH OPTIONS 62
FLASH EXPORT SETTINGS 63
MP3 SOUND 63
PUBLISHING TO AN OLDER VERSION OF FLASH 63
HTML SETTINGS 64
CREATING A FULL PAGE WEB SITE WITH FLASH 64
JUST A COUPLE OF CLICKS AND ITS READY FOR THE WEB 65
EXPORTING FLASH USING THE ANIMATED GIF FORMAT 65
ANIMATED GIF FEATURES 66
USING FLASH HELP 66

EXPORTING & SAVING FOR THE WEB

PUBLISH SWF FILES FOR DISTRIBUTION ON THE WEB.

PUBLISH OPTIONS

❑ Open an animation to export as a Flash .SWF web document.

❑ Save the File to the location you want to create the Flash web movie file. *This is an interesting Flash oddity, you cannot set the save location in the publish dialog. The save location is based on the location where you saved the original Flash document.*

❑ Choose File-Publish-**SETTINGS** to get the following dialog box.

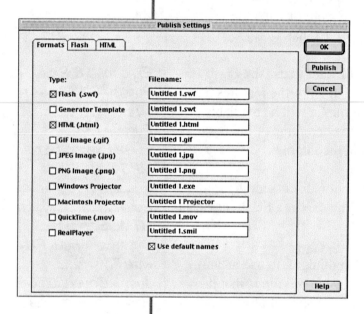

Looks intimidating but it is actually an easy to use tool.

Click on the items you want to create. By default Flash will create a SWF (Flash web movie file) and an HTML web page to access the SWF file.
Note that you can create a image file, QT movie, or a projector, in case you want to display the animation locally on your computer.

❑ Make sure Flash SWF and HTML are selected. For this project, make sure the other options are turned off.

❑ Click on the Flash tab to view additional Flash movie settings.

Load Order sets which layer will be loaded and viewed first. Since we most often create from the bottom this is the default, but if your time line starts at an upper layer you may want to choose Top down.

Generate size report is a great feature because it generates a text file that tells you frame by frame how much information is being downloaded. Great information to know if you need to revise your animation to better accommodate modem users.

Omit Trace Actions prevents the output window from opening and display comments that would be used to debug ActionScripts

Protect from Import prevents others from importing your Flash movie from the web and converting it back into an editable Flash file.

❑ Turn on the Protect from Import option.

Debugging Permitted turns on the debugger to allow debugging a Flash movie over the internet. If this option is selected then you should password-protect your movie file.

JPEG quality to squeeze it down, and make the imported Photoshop images smaller.

Flash also includes MP3 which is wonderful compression for your audio files. Unless you are familiar with audio and the advantages of MP3, I suggest using the default settings.

Version is a useful feature but beware if you save into an older version your may loose some of the ActionScript features and capabilities that you created in your animation.

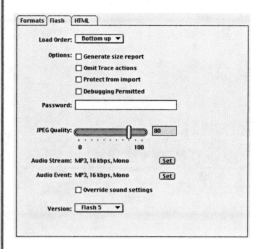

MP3 SOUND

PUBLISHING TO AN OLDER VERSION OF FLASH

HTML Settings

HTML determines the code and features that will be used within the HTML file that Flash will generate with your movie. If you are planning to imbed this movie into a GoLive or DreamWeaver document some of these features may not be relevant

Creating a Full Page Web Site with Flash

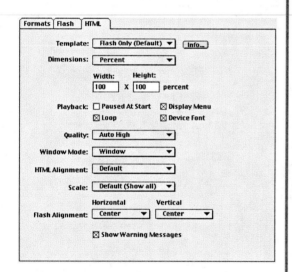

❑ Click on the template menu and work your way through the list of options. *Once an option is selected click on the Info button to see how it will display in the browser.* After you have reviewed the options, select the Flash Only (Default).

Template: [Flash Only (Default) ▼]

Dimensions: The default is Match movie, but you can also set movie dimensions in pixels or percent.
❑ Set Dimensions to Match Movie.

Want your Flash movie to fill your entire web page? Set the Dimensions to Percent and set the width and height to 100%. This not only makes your Flash movie fill the HTML document but when the user resizes the web document it resizes your Flash Movie.

Display Menu displays a shortcut menu when users right-click (Windows) or Control-clicks (Macintosh) the movie when viewed on the web.

Click on the Help button to see some of the other features. Take a look at the quality settings, this is a really cool feature and something you will want to consider based on who you think will be looking at this movie and the content.

❑ Set the quality setting to AutoHigh. *(This is a good option. It emphasizes image quality, but will drop the quality if the users playback speed is to slow or creating pauses in playback.*
If you don't like the results on AutoHigh then try Auto Low which emphasizes fast playback at the expense of image quality, but improves appearance if the users computer can handle it.
Leave other settings at the Default unless you have read the help file.

❑ Click on the Publish button. This will save the HTML file and the SWF file to the same location that you saved your native Flash file.

Creating SWF files is actually pretty easy!

Creating an Animated GIF with Flash.

❑ Open a simple animation. Choose something small because GIF"s can consume a lot of space.

❑ Choose File-**Export**-**MOVIE**

❑ In the Export dialog select the Animated GIF format. *(Choose the location you want to save your GIF.)*

JUST A COUPLE OF CLICKS AND ITS READY FOR THE WEB

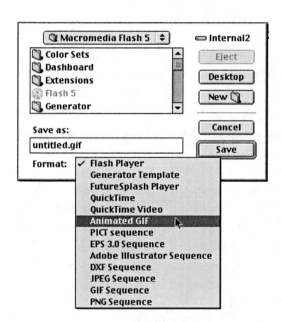

❑ In the Export GIF dialog, you can set the width height and resolution. *One of the things I like about Flash and the export GIF is that it is pretty straight forward and easy to use.*

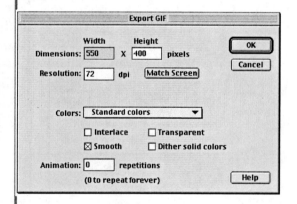

❑ Hit the Save button and you are done. That's it. They make it too easy!! *Your flash animation is saved as an animated GIF.*

I would like to see the option to limit the number of frames in my animated GIF. We could reduce the size if we used every 2nd, 3rd, or 4th frame, instead of creating a GIF file with all of the frames. (Director does this) but, hey, that is a small issue.

ANIMATED GIF FEATURES

Interlace: Allows the user to see a blurry preview before the full image is downloaded. Doesn't make much sense, for a GIF animation.

Transparent: White becomes transparent in the browser (to bad we can't choose a color for this one).

Smooth: produces anti-alaising, this is a great feature, use it.

Dither Solid Colors: I don't suggest using this one.

Colors:	Black & White
	4 colors
	8 colors
	16 colors
	32 colors
	64 colors
Animation:	128 colors
	256 colors
	Standard colors

Colors: In addition Flash allows you to reduce the color depth of the animated GIF which also helps to reduce the file size. If you can live with 128 or even 64 colors it will help to make your animated GIF much smaller.

USING FLASH HELP

This is a good time to mention the wonderful help features that are built into Flash. There will be a number of questions about what a particular button does that this book may not address. While working through these tutorials I strongly encourage you to select the Help button, which will launch you directly into a feature by feature discussion of the various options available in Flash.

The Help options do require that you have an internet browser such as Netscape or Internet Explorer, but you do NOT need to be connected to the web, as the web pages load locally.

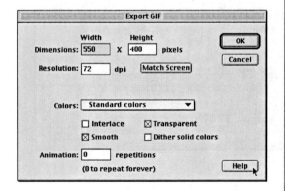

The best feature about the help buttons is that they are context sensitive. If you are looking at the Export GIF dialog box and select Help, it will open up pages related to the Export GIF options.

CHAPTER 12

Interactivity with Buttons

Flash has only three types of symbols. They are graphics, buttons, and movieclips. While graphic symbols are pretty basic buttons open the door into Flash interactivity.

Buttons are the foundation of interactivity without programming in Flash. This is one of the biggest secrets of Flash. Many Flash users never grasp the difference between a HTML type web page button and a Flash button. A web button is something you click on, a Flash button offers a doorway to mesmerizing web interactivity. When you get to chapters 19-22 you will see what I mean.

This chapter will show a simple rollover but later chapters will explore some of the power-user techniques and effects that you may have seen on the web. These were created using buttons inside movieclips, or movieclips inside buttons.

A rollover is pretty basic stuff, especially if you have been creating HTML based web pages. A rollover is basically having a new image appear when you roll over an object that is defined as a button. If you have worked in either GoLive or DreamWeaver you had to make your rollover image the same size as the button in the "normal" state. This is not the case in Flash. Your rollover image can be as large or as small as you want it to be. When a user rolls over a button it could change the entire appearance of the stage. Rolling over a button can present text, sounds, music, images or a combination of these. But even better than that, the button

Topics

BUTTONS CAN CHANGE THE STAGE . 67
THE SECRET OF FLASH 67
BUTTON OBJECTS ARE ESSENTIAL FOR
CREATING GAMES. 68
PROJECT 69
CONVERTING TO A BUTTON SYMBOL 69
THE BUTTON SYMBOL EDITOR 70
BUTTON STATES 70
CREATE BUTTON STATES.............. 71
TESTING THE BUTTON 71
CREATING AN OVER STATE. 71
CREATING A DOWN STATE. 72
CREATE BUTTON STATES.............. 72
THE HIT STATE 73
FURTHER EXPLORATION 74

THE SECRET OF FLASH

BUTTONS CAN CHANGE THE ENTIRE STAGE

Button Objects are Essential for Creating Games.

itself can be an animation and when the user rolls over it can change how the animation plays. A button can also be scripted to behave in a specified way and also make decisions based on what is happening in the movie.

This is a interesting concept to toy with and one that a some developers have utilized with really incredible effect.

A couple of my students developed a on-line game where the button was an animation of a plane flying across the screen. When the user click on the plane they would hear and see the explosion and then the plane would vanish. We could make the game even more difficult by having the plane dodge out of the way when the user rolls over it.

A while back, I was working with Flash 4 scripting to explore ways to keep score for an arcade style game. I created a button that was an animation of a bunny jumping up and down. The "bunny button" would run across the stage while the user attempted to shoot. When the user rolled over the "bunny button" the bunny would try to escape and would also appear as though it where a target in a hunters gun sight. When the user successfully fired the gun at, and struck the bunny, the bunny button would perform a forward flip through the air, while yelling "Yahoo", then fall on the stage with a "Wump" sound. As you can see, a button in Flash is not just something to click on. It is a part of the Flash tool palette that allows us to create incredibly involved and complex interaction.

The next couple of chapters will explore using buttons to control Flash animation, create interactive web portfolios by offering users a choice about the content they wish to see, and provide users with control over sound for web playback.

This tutorial will take you through the basics of creating interactivity through the use of buttons in

Flash. As you have already experienced in the previous lessons, the graphics and project are basic in order to allow you to quickly gain the concepts. Your mission is to take this basic information and apply your own imagination and creativity. Exploration is the key.

❑ Create a new Flash document and create a circle object on the stage that has no line and is filled with the color red.

❑ Convert the object into a symbol. *With the pointer tool* 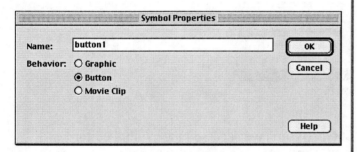 *select the object and choose Insert-Convert to Symbol.*

❑ In the Symbol Properties dialog name this object "button 1" and set the behavior to "Button". (See diagram below)

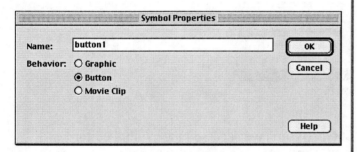

❑ Click OK to exit the Symbol Properties dialog box.

A button symbol is similar to a graphic symbol, in that you can reuse it many times during the animation. What makes a button symbol different is that when the user moves the cursor over the button it can change appearance, and when the user clicks on the button it can further change appearance. Of the three symbols (graphic, button, and movieclip) the button is the only symbol that can respond to a mouse event, such as a mouse click. This becomes important when you want to use ActionScript to respond to the users actions.

CONVERTING AN OBJECT INTO A BUTTON SYMBOL

ENTERING THE BUTTON SYMBOL EDITOR

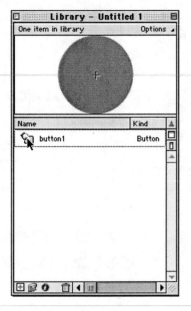

FLASH BUTTON STATES

❑ To access the symbol editor for the button, display the Library palette (Window-Library) and double click on the icon for button1.
Shown in the diagram.
Note: If you double click on the WORD "button 1", the Library palette will allow you to change the name of the symbol. If you double click on the button ICON in the Library palette, you will enter the symbol editor.

One way to be certain that you are in the symbol editor is by looking in the upper left corner of the Flash window. In the example shown below Scene 1 is available but inactive. "button 1" is active and available for editing. IF you wanted to return to editing the movie you could click on Scene 1, which would take you out of the symbol editor. Another way to exit the scene editor is to choose Edit Movie from the Edit menu.

❑ Once you have accessed the symbol editor for "button 1" take a look at the what has replaced the timeline. Instead of a timeline you are presented with button states.

*When producing content for the web a button can have three different types of display (or STATES). The **Up state** is what the button looks like when nothing is happening to it. The cursor is NOT over the button.*
*The **Over state** is how the button will appear when the cursor is moved on top of the button.*
*The **Down state** is how the button appears when the user "clicks" on the button.*

The Hit state defines the "hot spot" area of the button and is discussed in more detail at the end of this chapter.

For this project we will create an Over and Down state. By default Flash has a keyframe in the Up state but no keyframe in the other states.

❑ Click below the word "Over" to highlight the cell.

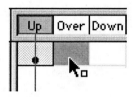

❑ With the Over state highlighted choose Insert-Blank Keyframe from the menu bar.

❑ With the Over state still selected, draw a square in the center of the stage. The square should be centered on the crosshair that appears on the stage.

❑ Choose Edit-Edit Movie to exit the symbol editor and return to the movie, or select the Scene1 button.

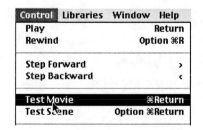

❑ Choose Control-**Test Movie** to see if the Over state works.

CREATING AN OVER STATE.

ADDING A BLANK KEYFRAMES TO CREATE BUTTON STATES

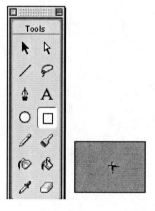

TESTING THE BUTTON

CREATING A DOWN STATE.

ADDING A KEYFRAMES TO CREATE BUTTON STATES

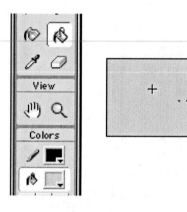

SAVE THIS PROJECT IT WILL BE USED IN THE NEXT SECTION

When you drag your cursor over the button object it should change from a circle to a square.

❑ Close the Test Movie window. Then using the Library palette double click on "button 1" to return to the symbol editor for Button1.

❑ Once you are back in the symbol editor, click on the Down state in the timeline.

❑ Choose **Insert-Keyframe** to make the DOWN state active.

Note: Choosing Insert-Keframe copies the contents from the previous keyframe, Insert-BLANK Keyframe provides a blank stage to create from scratch.

❑ Select the paint bucket from the tool palette, set the color to yellow, and fill the square with the new color.

❑ Exit the symbol editor. Choose Edit-Edit Movie to exit the symbol editor and return to the movie, or select the Scene1 button.

❑ Choose Control-Test Movie to see if the Over state works.
When you drag your cursor over the button it changes into a square when you click on the button object it changes color.

❑ Save a copy of this Flash animation, it will be used in the next project, on adding Action Scripts to a Flash button.

Understanding the Hit State.

The hit state is not required in all buttons but is absolutely essential for some. The hit state is an invisible area that we create that defines the hot spot of the button or to put it in other words the Hit State defines the "Active area" of a button.

For example, lets say your button is a round circle in the Up state, but when the user rolls over it changes into text that lets the user know what this button does. See example at right.

By default the Over state is only active as long as the tip of the cursor is touching the button. (or in this case, touching a letter.)

In another example, maybe the button explodes in the Over state. Because the pieces of the button are no longer under the cursor the Over state cannot become active.

To resolve this problem we create a hit state that defines the hot spot area of the button.

In the examples discussed, we would insert a keyframe into the Down state then insert a blank keyframe into the Hit state. Using the circle or the square tool, draw a shape that will represent the buttons hot spot. The color of the object drawn in the Hit state is not important because the hit state graphic is never seen by the user. The hit state only defines the active area of the button.

The shape drawn into the hit state never shows up on the stage, but now when the user drags the cursor into the Hot Spot area that was defined by the Hit state, the button changes.

Normal State

Over State

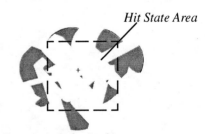

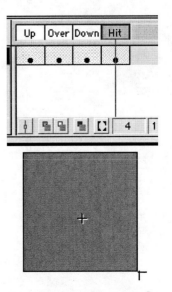

Hit State Area

Button explodes in the over state

FURTHER EXPLORATION

Further Experimentation:
Use a copy of this Flash movie. Keep the original, it will be used in the next section of this chapter.

To get more comfortable with Flash button states experiment with some of the following...

❑ Create a button that changes from a sad face into a happy face when the user rolls over.

❑ Create a button that displays text information in the over state.

❑ Import two scanned photos and have the images change when the user rolls over.

❑ Add depth to your images. Import a greyscale and color copy of your image. Have the greyscale image display in the Up state and the Color image display in the Over state.

❑ Create an Over state that is large enough to cover the entire stage, so when the user rolls over the button the stage appears to change. Note: you could also do this with a large image in the Over state.

❑ Create a button with an Over state, then use it in tweened animation. Have the button change color and fade over time as it moves across the stage. Note how the tweening effects change the Over state and the Down state you created.

❑ Using the Options-Pop-out menu on the Library palette, make several copies of the button. Edit each one so they look different in the Over state. Add a couple of layers to your movie-timeline and have each button animate in different direction when the movie is played.

❑ See if you can create a new animation where the object breaks apart when the user rolls over it, then comes back together in the Down state.

CHAPTER 13

Connecting to the Web

This example will use the button created in the previous chapter to open a web page on the internet.

❑ Once you have created a button symbol and given it an Over state and a Down state the next task is to have it actually do something. This project will use Flash buttons and ActionScript to connect to other web pages. *(If you did not complete the previous chapter then create a button symbol with an over and down state and place it on the stage.)*

❑ Clear the stage. Delete any objects from the stage. Trash any extra layers in the timeline.

❑ Choose Window-PanelSets-DefaultLayout to reset the palettes.

❑ Click once on frame 1 in the timeline, to make sure it is selected.

❑ Drag an "*instance*" (one copy) of the button from the library onto the stage.

❑ With the pointer tool, click one time on the button **on the stage**, to make sure it is selected.

The Instance palette appears in the lower right corner of your monitor.

❑ Select the Edit Actions button, on the Instance palette, as shown.

Topics

OBJECT ACTIONS WINDOW 76
CAPTURING MOUSE EVENTS 76
CONNECT TO WEB PAGE ACTION ... 77
WHERE CAN ACTIONSCRIPTS BE
APPLIED? 77
LINKING TO PAGES LOCALLY 77
PREVIEW IN BROWSER 78
ADDITIONAL EXPERIMENTATION 78

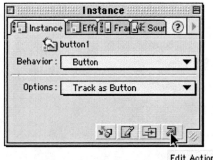

OBJECT ACTIONS WINDOW

No action selected.

No Parameters.

❏ The Object Actions window is displayed.
(If you see Frame Actions then close the window and repeat the previous three steps.)

❏ In the upper right corner of the Object Actions window click the pop-out menu to make sure the Normal Mode is selected.

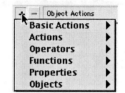

❏ Click the plus (+) button to see some of the commands available, as shown above.

The action that we want, is to have the user connect to another page. The trigger for this event will be when the user releases the button.

CAPTURING MOUSE EVENTS

❏ Select the "on" action, as shown below.

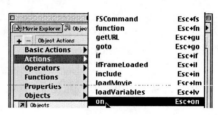

The Object Actions palette with the "on" command displayed.

Available ActionScript commands

Note: That you can capture a variety of events using the "on" action.

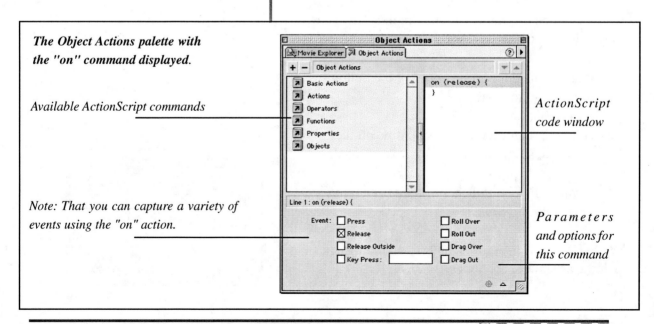

ActionScript code window

Parameters and options for this command

The next part of the script is what we want to happen after the user releases the button

❑ Select the plus (+) symbol and choose Basic Actions-Get URL.

❑ Issuing this command provides options at the bottom of the Object Actions dialog where you can type in the http address.
Type in "http://hotFlashBook.com"

Notes about the Get URL action:

1. You created the Get URL action in a two step process. First define the event that triggers the action then create the action. If you would have first selected the Get URL command, Flash would have automatically defined the "on" event for you.

2. In this example you are linking to a web address on the web, but you can also make relative links in Flash. For example, if you had a page in your site folder called "my.html" you would enter "my.html" in the URL space.

URL : |my.html

Just as with HTML, a relative address means that the Flash SWF file and the HTML file must be in the same folder.

3. In this project we applied the ActionScript behavior to one instance of the button on the stage using an object action. If you were to drag another instance of the button onto the stage it would not have any ActionScripting. This is actually to your benefit because you can invest time in creating one really cool button, then drag several instances of it onto the stage and set a different web address for each instance of the button.

❑ Close the action palette.

You will need to preview this movie in a browser because the Test-Movie command will not perform the Get URL function.

CONNECT TO WEB PAGE ACTION

LINKING TO PAGES LOCALLY

WHERE CAN ACTIONSCRIPTS BE APPLIED?

Flash allows the use of ActionScript in two primary areas. You can apply Actions to an object on the stage or to a frame in the timeline.

PREVIEW IN BROWSER

To preview the movie using your browser.

❑ Launch a browser on your computer. Either Netscape or IE are fine.

❑ Choose File-Publish Preview-Default-(HTML) *This will launch the movie into the active browser and allow you to test the button to see if it works.*

File	Edit	View	Insert	Modify	Control	Libraries	Window
New				⌘N			Untitled
Open...				⌘O			
Open as Library...			Shift ⌘O				
Close				⌘W		10 15 20 25	
Save				⌘S			
Save As...			Shift ⌘S				
Revert							
Import...				⌘R		1 12.0 0.0s	
Export Movie...		Option Shift ⌘S					
Export Image...							
Publish Settings...		Shift ⌘F12					
Publish Preview			▶	Default – (HTML) F12			
Publish			Shift F12	Flash			
				HTML			

Problems? If you are unable to link to the page listed in the Get URL command then check to make sure you are connected to the internet, and that you typed the URL in correctly.

ADDITIONAL EXPERIMENTATION

Additional Experiments:

❑ Create three more instances of your button symbol on the stage and set each instance to link to a different web page.

❑ Try creating an interactive web game where the user must click moving animated buttons to access different web sites.

❑ Create a Flash Animation that allows users to connect to different Flash animations in your existing web site.

❑ Take a Photo of your face, and then select the eyes, convert them into button symbols. Make the eyes change color during Over state. Have them link to a web page that allows the user to see inside your mind.

CHAPTER 14

Controlling Animation with ActionScript

Letting the user control the animation.

Allowing the user an opportunity to control the animation not only involves the user in the viewing process but also makes the animation more entertaining.

For this project we'll place three buttons in an animation that allows the user to stop, start, and restart the animation as desired. This project provides additional experience with buttons, and introduces some very basic, and easy to use ActionScript. In the further exploration section, at the end of this project, there is some code that can be used to create a rewind or step back button.

If you previously created the Solar Explosion then open a copy of that file. If you did not try the Solar Explosion then open any animation that is longer then 30 frames.

❑ Open an previously created animation that is at least 30 frames in length.

❑ Choose Window-Panel Sets-Default Layout to reset the palettes.

Panel Sets ▶ **Default Layout**

Topics

ABOUT THIS PROJECT 79
SETUP 79
CREATING A BUTTON SYMBOL 80
ACCESSING ACTIONSCRIPT 80
CREATING A STOP SCRIPT 81
VIEWING THE SCRIPT 81
TESTING THE SCRIPT 81
ADDING INSTANCES OF A BUTTON .. 82
CREATING A PLAY SCRIPT 82
SCRIPTING THE RESTART BUTTON .. 83
GOTO SCRIPT OPTIONS 83
FURTHER EXPLORATION 84

ABOUT THIS PROJECT

SETUP

❏ Create a new layer (in your existing animation) and click on frame 1 in the new layer. *(By default the new layer will extend the full length of your existing animation timeline.)*

In the next few steps you will create a button symbol.

❏ Draw a square on the stage.

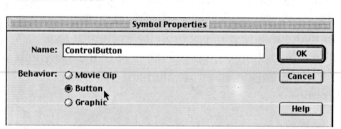

❏ Select the square, and choose Insert-Convert to Symbol.

❏ Select the button option and call it "ControlButton".

CREATING A BUTTON SYMBOL

Symbol Properties	
Name: ControlButton	OK
Behavior: ◯ Movie Clip	Cancel
⦿ Button	
◯ Graphic	Help

❏ With the button still selected, choose the Edit Actions button from the Instance palette, see diagram. This will display the Object Actions palette. *(The Instance palette is located in the lower right corner of your monitor.)*

ACCESSING ACTIONSCRIPT

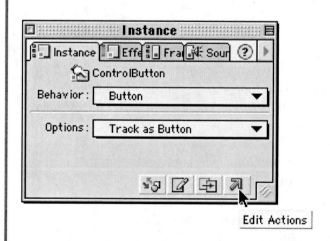

© KALDAHL

❏ In the object actions dialog box you will see two windows. The one on the left displays a list of commands and the one on the right will show the ActionScripting programming code.

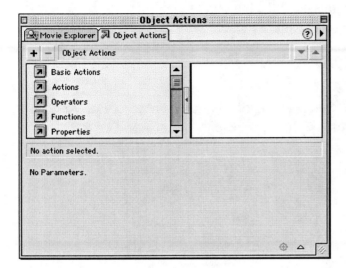

❏ Click the Basic Actions icon to display the basic commands.

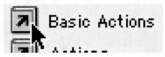

❏ Double click on the Stop command.

❏ You should see the following code appear in the code window.

```
on (release) {
stop ();
}
```

❏ Close the Object Actions dialog.

❏ Choose the text tool and type the word "Stop" on top of the button.

❏ Choose Control-Test Movie to see how the button works. *During the animation when you click on the stop button it should stop the animation.*

CREATING A STOP SCRIPT

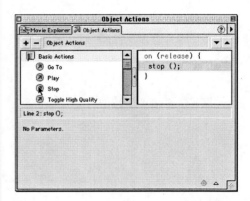

VIEWING THE SCRIPT

TESTING THE SCRIPT

ADDING INSTANCES OF THE MASTER BUTTON

CREATING A PLAY SCRIPT

Great Huh?? But once stopped it gets kinda boring.
We need a "Go" button.
While we are at it lets add a "Replay" button.

❑ Open the Library palette and drag two more instances of the button onto the stage.
Set them side by side.

❑ Select the middle button then select Edit Actions from the Instance palette.

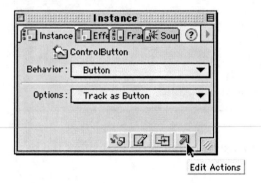

❑ In the Object Actions dialog, open Basic Actions and double click on the Play action.

The code window should display the following

```
on (release) {
 play ();
 }
```

❑ Close 🗅 the Object Actions dialog.

❏ Select the third button on the stage and again choose Edit Actions from the Instance dialog.

❏ Double click on the "Go To" action from Basic Actions

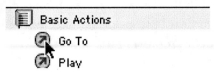

❏ The GoTo action has options which are displayed in the bottom of the Object Actions dialog. The default should look like the diagram shown. (if not make any changes required to match the diagram)

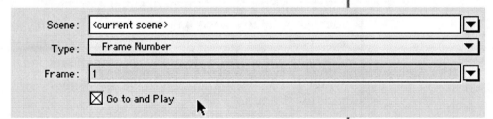

❏ The code window should display the following. What the code says is that when the user releases the button, the movie will go to and play frame 1. This is our restart button.

```
on (release) {
  gotoAndPlay (1);
}
```

❏ Close 🗖 the Object Actions dialog.

❏ Use the text tool to label the middle button, "GO", and label the end button "Restart".

Stop   Go   Restart

❏ Use Control-Test Movie to see if the buttons are working properly.
These are some of the basic actions provided by ActionScript that make your web content more compelling to users, and represents one of the reasons why Flash is becoming so popular on the web. The following are some projects you might

FURTHER EXPLORATION

Come up with creative buttons.

consider to enhance the actions or further the options Flash's actions provide.

1. Work in Flash to create graphics buttons that show a greater level of sophistication than the examples provided in this project. If you look on the web some of the coolest buttons do not use text but instead use symbols to represent the actions.
At the time of this writing the trend in web design is to produce small buttons, that are interesting, visually compelling and unobtrusive.
The goal is not to produce buttons for a single animation but to design buttons that can be used throughout your site.

2. Create a Step Back / Rewind button. For those of you who want to get more involved in the scripting aspects of Flash, create a new button and insert the following code. This code produces a simple rewind button. Each time the user clicks the movie steps back five frames.

```
on (press) {
  gotoAndPlay (_currentframe-5);
}
```

Ideally, we would want the rewind button to keep rewinding as long as the user holds the rewind button down. I have experimented with a couple of simple ActionScripts dropped into the parent movie that did not work. The only way, that I have been able to find, to have the rewind button continue to rewind is by placing the rewind statement into a movieclip and utilizing the independent timeline provided by a movieclip to repeat the statement. This actually offers an advantage, because the movieclip is self contained and can be dropped into any movie.
If you are able to come up with a ActionScript, that rewinds while the mouse button is held down, **without using a movieclip**, email me and you will not only win my respect and admiration but I will publish your solution and credit you as the developer on my web site and in the next edition of this book.

CHAPTER 15

Interactive Web Portfolio with ActionScript

Using button and frame ActionScript to provide user choices.

Sometimes you want a movie to stop at a certain point and let the user choose between a couple of different options. As a graphic artist, you might want to display several images of your work. Rather than forcing the user to see them sequentially, you might want to allow the user to choose the image (or animation) they are most interested in and click a button to see it. Then offer a button to return to a navigation point and select from other images.

This project will begin with a very basic intro scene, then present the user with a choice of two different buttons for navigation. Once you have completed this project you should easily be able to adapt this example to suit the needs of your own web presentation.

The graphics and examples used in this project are very basic. My goal, for this project, is to show you how to create navigation.

The project
❑ Launch Flash and create a new document.

Topics

THE PROJECT 85
CREATING THE INTRO SCENE 86
ZOOMING TYPE 86
ADDING USER NAVIGATION 87
INSERT DUMMY IMAGES 87
MASTER BUTTON SYMBOL 88
SEGMENTING THE MOVIE 88
ADDING NAVIGATION SCRIPTS 88
GO TO AND STOP SCRIPT 89
SCRIPTING THE SECOND BUTTON .. 89
CREATING A RETURN BUTTON 90
SCRIPTED BUTTON TO THE LIBRARY 91
REUSING A BUTTON SYMBOL 92
ADDING FRAME ACTIONS 93
TEST THE MOVIE 94
FURTHER EXPLORATION 94

About this project:
This project provides the user with navigation buttons. From frame 1-15 there is a short introductory animation. On frame 20 and frame 30 there are images for the user to see. The animation stops at frame 15 and waits for the user to choose which image they want to see. Frame 20 and 30 have navigation buttons to allow the user to return to frame 15.

THE PROJECT

CREATING THE INTRO SCENE

ZOOMING TYPE

❑ Choose Window-Panel Sets-Default Layout to rearrange the palettes.

Panel Sets ▶ **Default Layout**

❑ Select the text tool A from the tool palette.

❑ Select the Character palette to choose a font, Size and color. *(36-48 point type should be fine)*

❑ Click on the stage to set the insertion point and type in the word "Welcome".

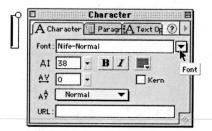

❑ Select frame 15 on the timeline and insert a keyframe.

Insert Keyframe

❑ Select frame 1 on the timeline.

❑ With the pointer tool ▲ selected choose the resize option from the tool palette 🔄 and make the type small.

❑ With frame 1 still selected, choose the Frame palette and create a motion tween.

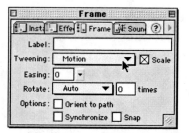

The type will now grow from frame 1 - 15.

❏ Select frame 20 and insert a **blank**-keyframe.

❏ On frame 20 Draw a circle.

❏ Select frame 30 and insert a **blank**-keyframe.

❏ On frame 30 draw a square.

Your timeline should now look like the example shown.
A tween from frames 1-15, a circle on frame 20 and a square on frame 30.
(Note: I've added labels, using the Frame palette, to make the illustration clearer, .)

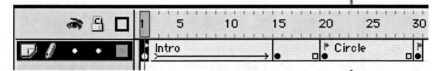

❏ Use Control-Test movie to see what it does.
The movie should begin with growing type, then show the circle, then flash the square, briefly, before looping back to the growing type.
OK, so this movie is not going to win any animation awards but it does provide a framework for future projects you may want to produce.

Adding User Interaction and Control
❏ Add a new layer to the timeline.

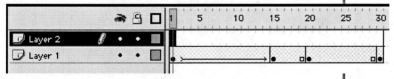

The new layer will be used to add navigation buttons.

❏ Select frame 1 of the new layer and draw a square on the stage. It will be used as a navigation button.

INSERT DUMMY IMAGES

Note: In order to keep this project from becoming too long we will use simple objects. Once completed you can easily revise this movie and insert your own artwork on frames 20 and 30.

ADDING USER NAVIGATION

CREATING THE MASTER BUTTON SYMBOL

❏ Click on frame 1 in the **new layer** (to select the button) then choose Insert-Convert to Symbol.

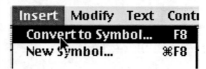

❏ In the symbol window, set the behavior to Button, and name this symbol "NavButton" then choose OK to close the Symbol Properties window. *Now that you have created a button symbol, stored in the library for later use.*

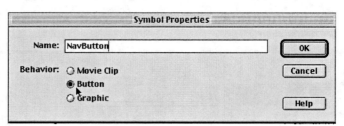

SEGMENTING THE MOVIE

❏ Select and delete the button from the stage.

❏ On layer 2 (the new layer) insert a **blank**-keyframe at frame 15, 20, and 30.

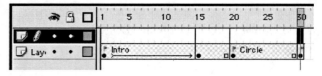

ADDING NAVIGATION SCRIPTS TO THE BUTTONS

❏ Select frame 15, on layer 2, on the timeline, open the Library palette and drag 2 instances of the "NavButton" onto the stage.

❏ Click once on the first button, then select the Instance palette, and select the Edit Action button. This will bring up the ActionScript dialog box.

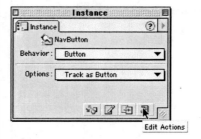

❑ Under Basic Actions, double click the "Go To" action.

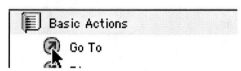

❑ In the lower part of the ActionScript dialog set the parameters to the following.
Choose frame 20 as the frame to Go To and turn **off** the "Go to and Play" option.
This tells Flash to Go To and Stop on frame 20.

Line 2: gotoAndStop (20);	
Scene:	<current scene> ▼
Type:	Frame Number ▼
Frame:	20 ▼
	☐ Go to and Play

The script window should display the following.

```
on (release) {
  gotoAndStop (20);
}
```

❑ Close the ActionScript dialog, then select the second button. In the Instance palette select the Edit Action button to display the Scripting dialog box.

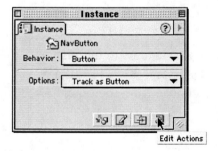

❑ Under Basic Actions, double click the "Go To" action.

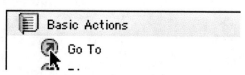

❑ In the lower part of the Actions dialog set the parameters to the following.
Choose frame 30 as the frame to "Go To", and turn OFF the "Go to and Play" option.

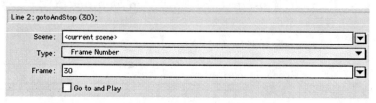

The Script window should display the following.

```
on (release) {
    gotoAndStop (30);
}
```

The script says that when the user releases the button, the movie will jump to frame 30, square, and stop the movie.

❑ Close the ActionScript dialog and select the text tool. Place the word "Circle" on the first button. Place the word "Square" on the second button.

Now that we have buttons to take us to the images (or animations) at frames 20 and 30, we need a way to return to frame 15 to choose from the other options.

❑ Select frame 20, on layer 2, of the timeline, and drag another instance of the NavButton from the Library palette onto the stage.

CREATING A RETURN BUTTON

❑ Select the new Navbutton, on the stage, then select the Instance palette, and select the Edit Action button. *This will bring up the scripting window.*

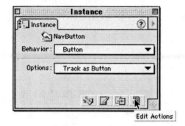

❑ Under Basic Actions, double click the "Go To" action.

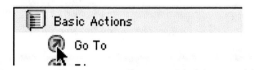

❑ In the lower part of the actions wondow set the parameters to the following.
Choose frame 15 as the frame to "Go To" and turn off the "Go to and Play" Button.

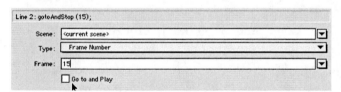

The Script window should display the following.

```
on (release) {
  gotoAndStop (15);
}
```

By now you have probably realized that this script tells the playback head to return to frame 15 and to stop the movie, waiting for the user to select a different button.

❑ Close the script window, select the text tool, and place text on the button that says "Return".

You now have a button that returns the user to frame 15.

ADDING A SCRIPTED BUTTON TO THE LIBRARY

At this point you have added buttons on frame 15 to navigate to either the circle(20) or the square(30). You have also, just created a button that will return the user to frame 15. We now need a button to return the user from frame 30. Rather than create a new button from scratch, we can re-use the button we have already created.

REUSING A BUTTON SYMBOL

❑ With the button on frame 20, of layer 2 still selected, use the pointer tool select both the button and the text. With both selected choose the menu Insert-Convert to Symbol. Name this button symbol "ReturnFrame15". Make sure the Button option is selected in the Symbol Properties dialog, then choose OK to save it.

To select both the button and text: Choose the pointer tool from the tool palette and drag around the button to select the text and the button.

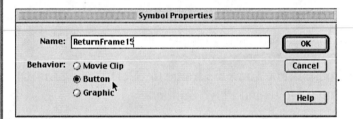

❑ Click on frame 30 on the timeline and drag a copy of the " ReturnFrame15" button onto the stage. *Not only is the button and the text copied in the symbol, but the ActionScript is copied as well.*

If you were to test the movie at this point it would display the buttons but would loop from frame 1-30 without ever stopping. The final step for this movie is to tell it to stop on frame 15 and wait for the user to select from the navigation buttons.

❑ Add a new layer to this movie.

❑ Select frame 15, in the new layer and add a keyframe.

Insert Keyframe

❑ Double click on frame 15 (on the new layer) to display the Frames Actions palette.

❑ In the left window of the Frames Actions palette, select Basic Actions- and double click on the Stop command.

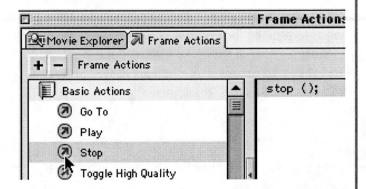

❑ The script window will now display stop (); *This stop command will only be active when the movie hits the keyframe 15 which has the Stop command applied.*

❑ Choose Control-Test Movie to see if the frame and button actions are working properly.

If all went well then the movie should load, play, and STOP on frame 15. Based on the users choice, the movie will either go to (and stop) on either the circle (frame 20) or the Square (frame 30).

Your final timeline should resemble the following illustration. Layer 1 holds the animation and images, and it has keyframes at frame 15, 20, and 30. Layer 2, which contains the navigation buttons, has keyframes at frame 15, 20, and 30. Frame 15 offers 2 choices (circle or square) frames 20 and 30 have return buttons. Layer 3, has a keyframe at frame 15, which contains the frame script that tells the animation to stop and wait for user interaction.

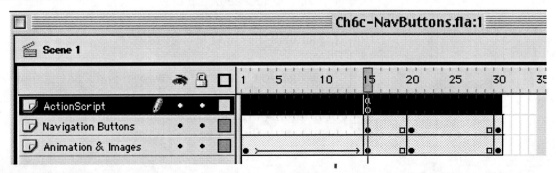

TEST THE MOVIE

FURTHER EXPLORATION

When the user clicks on the return button the movie should return to, and stop, on frame 15 and wait for the user to make another selection.

This project was fairly involved. You should be able to recycle this project, and the actions, for use with your own images or animations without a huge amount of modification. Simply import your own images to replace the circle and square. I'm sure that you have a grasp of these navigation concepts and could easily add many more images to this project using frame 15 as the "main menu" or your portfolio.

Question:
Would this type of navigation be easier in a HTML document?

Answer:
If you already know HTML, and you are new to Flash then it is possible that HTML would be easier, if the images are static. If you want to add any type of animated effects, such as those discussed in later in this book, then HTML will not provide the same capabilities.

If you are a visual artist or photographer or designer glance at chapter 22, "Interactive Web for Photographers" to see how you can combine animation with visual interactivity to create a stunning web presentation!

Further Exploration:

Create a new movie, (or use this project) import 3 images, (or use three animations) and create an opening sequence that includes navigation buttons to allow the user to navigate to each of the 3 images (or animations) in your portfolio.

Now that you have the framework, and a navigation button that returns the user to frame 15 (where the user can make a choice) within minutes you should be able to create a vast web portfolio.

CHAPTER 16

Sound & Buttons

Adding Sound to Flash

Flash can utilize sound in a couple of different ways. A sound can be set to play or loop in the background. With Flash (or Director) we can give users an opportunity to turn the sound off, lower the volume or even provide the user with a couple of different sounds and allow them to create their own mix! Sound can also be triggered when a particular frame is encountered. This project will demonstrate how sound can be triggered by an event such as a mouse over a button or a mouse down on a button.

In this project you'll add a sound to the over state and to the down sate of a button.

❑ Create a simple animation, Flash movie, with a button symbol on the stage. *If you want you might create an over and a down state for the button.*

❑ Use Control-Test Movie to make sure the button works.

❑ Import two sound files into the movie by choosing File-Import. Select a sound that represents a "mouse click" and a sound to be used when the mouse is over the button.

■ If you do not have sound files you can find a few sample sounds in the Flash Common Library. Choose Window-Common Library - Sounds.

Topics

SOUND IMPORT PROBLEMS 96
TESTING SOUNDS IN FLASH 96
SOUND TO THE OVER STATE 96
SOUND TO THE DOWN STATE 96

For this project you will need *a couple of basic sound files. A mousedown "click" sound and a mouse over "wrrr" sound, saved in either the ".AIF" file or ".WAVE" file formats. If you do not have sound files you can use the samples sounds provided in the Flash Common Library.*

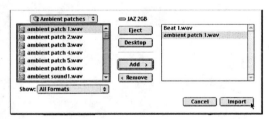

Import dialog box with 2 sounds selected for import.

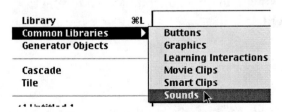

SOUND IMPORT PROBLEMS

Play Button

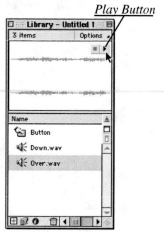

TESTING SOUNDS IN FLASH

ADDING SOUND TO THE OVER STATE

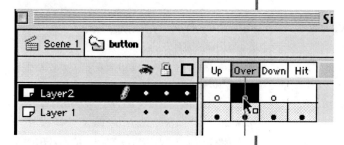

ADDING SOUND TO THE DOWN STATE

Note: It is a good idea to have a sound editing utility, such as Peak. Flash is fussy and if the sound has any type of compression applied, Flash will refuse to import the file. If Flash refuses to import your sound file I open it in Peak (or some other sound editing application) and to save it uncompressed in either the AIF or WAVE file format. This fixes the problem ninety nine percent of the time. If it cannot be opened in a sound editor I would assume the sound is corrupted.

❏ Open the Library palette to see the imported sounds.
You can preview/listen to the sounds by clicking on the play button in the library palette.

❏ Double click on the "button" in the Library palette, to enter the symbol editor for the button.

❏ Add a new layer to the button symbol.

❏ Add a keyframe to the Over and Down states on the new layer.

❏ With the Over state selected, in layer 2, drag the "over sound.wav" file onto the stage.

❏ With the Down state selected, in layer 2, drag the " down.wav " file onto the stage.

❏ Use Control-Test Movie to test the movie to see how it works.

If it works properly the over sound should play when you move the cursor over the button. When you click on the button, the down sound should play.

Adding sound to Flash buttons is easy. The real key is finding copyright free sounds (or creating your own) and saving them in an uncompressed format that Flash will accept.

CHAPTER 17

Controlling MP3 Sounds with Flash

If you have ever tried to add a sound to a web page using DreamWeaver or GoLive you know that it can be difficult. Between the two GoLive has better built in capabilities and does a nice job of starting the sound but there is always the question of whether or not the user will have a plug-in capable of reading, playing, and allowing sound control. I'm sure you have encountered pages where you heard some background music and initially found it enjoyable, but after a few minutes your were ready to leave the site just to stop the sound. Flash not only allows the option of providing user controls but also allows us to design how those controls will look in order to have them compliment the design of our web pages.

Why use Flash for your sounds? MP3 compression!! Need I say more? OK, customized interface that compliments your web site design. More, you say!! The ability to provide users with a choice of several sound tracks, and the ability to load multiple sounds in separate channels so the user can create their own sound mix. The choice of overlapping or streaming audio. As far as which plug-in to use for sound, the Flash plug-in is growing in popularity, supported by two major software vendors, Adobe and Macromedia, and it is easy to install a Flash sound in either GoLive or DreamWeaver. Flash also has the added benefit of being able to direct the user to Macromedia's plug-

Topics

FLASH FOR BACKGROUND SOUND . 105
CONCEPTS COVERED 106
ABOUT PROGRAMMING IN FLASH .. 106
COPYRIGHT ISSUES WITH SOUNDS 107
THE PROJECT 107
COPYRIGHT FREE SOUNDS 107
PROJECT SET-UP 108
ROLLOVER EFFECT FOR PNG 109
ADDING SOUND 110
FLASH INSTANCE SCRIPTING 111
STOP ALL SOUNDS SCRIPT 111
FURTHER EXPLORATION 112

WHY USE FLASH FOR BACKGROUND SOUNDS?

Concepts Covered

in download site, if the user does not have the plug-in installed. Since you are learning Flash it makes sense to focus on this plug-in to reduce the possibility of the user searching for plug-ins to access the content on your web site.

This, and the next project will cover a couple of different concepts.
1. Explore the use of sound in web creation.
2. Provide more experience with the creation and use of buttons.
3. Further the use of ActionScript.
4. Explore the use of a SWF file as a web page object.

About Programming in Flash

ActionScript programming, just as with any other programming language, requires a few qualities that not everyone has.
1. Tenacity, the ability to stick to a task, to work through problems and to maintain a level head when things don't work as expected. When dealing with lines of code this can be difficult.
2. Patience, this is probably the most essential ability one must have to work with computer programming.
3. Ingenuity. The ability to use your knowledge of the language when trying to solve a problem and to look for alternative workarounds or solutions when the first approach does not work.
4. The ability to think both logically and creatively, to see beyond the basics into the what-ifs.
On the other hand, Flash makes programming as painless and easy as possible. As you have already seen, Flash generates much of the basic code with just a couple clicks of a button.
I personally believe that the best way to learn about programming is with an application such as Flash or Director, especially for creative individuals. It allows you an opportunity to work visually and start simply. You may at times get frustrated with the precise nature of programming but I encourage you to perservere. In the long run you will find that programming opens a new and wonderful realm into how you can express your creativity.

Legal issues surrounding the use of Copyrighted music:
Can you use the MP3 files that you downloaded? Most likely the answer is "Not without permission" You might state "Hey, but I am a student learning to use Flash" and the response is, if you use a copyrighted sound and put that sound on your web site you have published someone else's work. As a student you most likely would be asked to discontinue your site, but as a professional producing a web site for a customer this is a critically important issue. You do not want to place your customer at risk for a lawsuit, this is a guaranteed way to lose your customers.

So how do you find sounds that you can use on your web site?

If you are musically inclined, you can create your own sounds. If you are producing work for a customer, this adds to the value of your services.

Another approach is to use some of the copyright free sounds that are available on the internet. You can try performing a search for copyright free .WAV or .AIF files.

Another option is to log onto
http://hotFlashBook.com
I will provide a small library of music loops and commonly used sounds for those of you who have purchased this book. I will also try to provide links to other sites that provide copyright free sound files.

The project:
In this project we will create a small simple Flash movie that can be dropped into an existing web page as a sound interface component. This file will contain sound compressed in the MP3 file format, and provides a button to allow the user to turn the sound off. One nice feature of this component is that it can be used repeatedly, and once completed, it is easy to change the sound file, if you want, to add this component to other web pages.

Before you begin this project you will want to create a button image that indicates it is the Sound-off button. The image you create should be no bigger than 50x50 pixels. You can create an image in Photoshop and save the image for web using the PNG format, or create the button in Flash. (See the tutorials at the end of this book on using Illustrator, and Photoshop to create and save graphics for Flash.)

Set-up

❏ Launch Flash and create a new document.

❏ Choose Window-Panel Sets-Default Layout to rearrange the palettes.

Panel Sets	▶	Default Layout

❏ If you do not already have a graphic, then create a graphic that will represent the Sound-off button. Remember it should be no larger than 50x50 pixels.

❏ If you created the button in any application other than Flash, choose File-Import and import the graphic into your Flash document. *(If Flash does not allow you to import the graphic then it was either saved in a file format that Flash will not accept, or the file has some form of corruption. Either way, open the original source file and re-save.)*

❏ If you are like me you will probably spend a lot more time creating the perfect graphic than you spend in Flash making it work.
The image shown below was created in Photoshop, and saved as a PNG-24 image with the transparency option turned on.

PROJECT SET-UP

❑ Use Modify-Movie and resize the movie to 50x50 pixels.

We want to keep the button small enough that it does not detract from the web page design but large enough that the user can spot it. Remember this button will eventually be used as one part of the final web page interface.

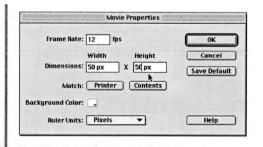

❑ If the button is not on the stage, drag it from the library onto the stage, and select it.

❑ Choose Insert-Convert to Symbol. Give the button the name "SoundOff" and set the behavior to Button.

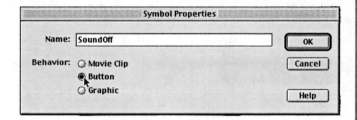

❑ If you have time you can experiment with adding an over and a down state for your button. *Note that if you imported a PNG, or transparent GIF, you may be able to add a glow to the outer edge in Flash, but you cannot change the color of the image itself. On the other hand you could create a separate image for the Normal, Over and Down state images in another application, import them, and apply them to the different button states. The example below shows a green glow around the edge of the button when in the Over state. A green glow was created using a radial gradient fill setting behind the transparent PNG button graphic and again, it only appears on the mouse Over state of the button.*

SIMPLE ROLLOVER EFFECT FOR PNG IMAGE

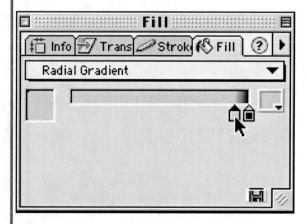

ADDING SOUND TO THE DOCUMENT:

The easiest way (without scripting) to add sound to a flash movie is to import it and drop it on the timeline. Using a short sound, you can loop it in order to have it continue to play.

❑ Choose File-Import to bring in your sound file. *Reminder: If you receive an error message when importing the sound file, it may have some form of compression. Open the sound file in a sound application and re-save it as either .AIF, or .WAV, then try importing again.*

❑ Create a new layer on the timeline, then drag the sound from the Library palette into frame 1 of the new layer.
(In the example below the sound is placed into layer 2)

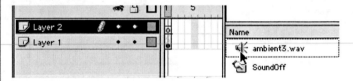

❑ On the Sound palette, select the imported sound, set the "Sync: to Start", and set the number of Loops: to 50.
(Why 50? After 50 times of hearing the same loop your user is ready for a break.)

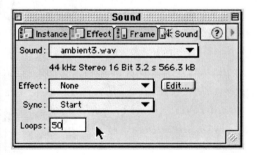

Quick Review:
At this point you have a small one frame movie that will play a sound that loops 50 times. The final element to be added is a short script for the button that stops the sound.

❑ Select the button on the stage, then choose the Instance palette.

❑ Click on the Edit Actions button on the Instance palette, to bring up the scripting window.

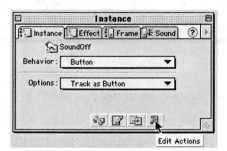

In the Object Actions dialog, choose the plus (+)-Basic Actions-Stop All Sounds. As shown in the diagram.

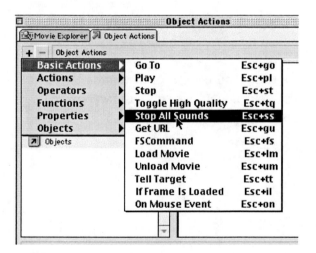

In the script portion of the Actions window you will see code that looks something like the following.

```
on (release) {
  stopAllSounds ();
}
```

This is a "Forgiving Button" because the action will not take place until the user releases the cursor over button. In this way if the user clicks on the button then changes their mind and moves the cursor off the button, the sound will not stop.

❑ Close the Object Actions window, choose Control-Test-Movie.

The user now has a way to turn the sound off. Unfortunately we have not provided them with a way to turn the sound back on. The next project in this book will explore this feature.

❑ Save this file.

❑ To use it on a web page you will need to publish it as a .SWF file.

Further Exploration

Further Exploration:

❑ Save a copy of this movie and import a new sound. Publish it as webSound2.swf

❑ Create a subtle animation for the button in order to draw the user's attention to it on the web page.

Controlling Sound With ActionScript

In order to make this applet even more useful, and to demonstrate how sound can be controlled, we will use ActionScript to activate a sound-on-button. With ActionScript we can control a sound without placing it on the timeline, as this project will demonstrate.

In this project you will create a small Flash movie, with embedded sound, that the user can turn on and off. It can be dropped an existing web page as a sound interface component or it can later be converted into a movieclip and reused in your flash projects. Once completed it will be a easy to change the sound file as needed.

Before you begin this project you will want to create a sound-off and a sound-on-button image. Each button should be no bigger than 50x50 pixels. If you choose to work in Photoshop, remember to Save-For-The-Web using the PNG-24 file format.

Set-up

❏ Launch Flash and create a new document.

Topics

PROJECT SETUP 97
SETUP CONTINUED 98
LINKING A LIBRARY SOUND 99
LINKAGE IDENTIFIER 99
THE PROJECT 99
SOUNDOFF BEHAVIOR 100
THE STOP SOUND SCRIPT 100
SCRIPTING THE ON BUTTON 101
PLAY LINKED LIBRARY SOUND 101
DISSECTING THE CODE 102
DEBUGGING CODE ERRORS 102
POSSIBLE SCRIPT ERRORS 103
ADDITIONAL EXPERIMENTATION 104

PROJECT SETUP

❑ Choose Window-Panel Sets-Default Layout.

Panel Sets	▶	Default Layout

❑ Use Modify-Movie and resize the movie to 50 pixels wide by 100 pixels tall. If your buttons are smaller, then make the movie smaller in order to take less space on the final web page.
We want to keep the button small enough that it does not detract from the web page design but large enough that the user can spot it.

❑ Create graphics that will represent the sound-off and a sound-on-button. Remember each should be no larger than 50 x 50 pixels.
If you created the button in any application other than Flash choose File-Import to import them. The buttons shown below were created in Flash.

❑ If the buttons are not on the stage, drag them from the library onto the stage.

❑ Convert the button graphics into button symbols. name the sound-off-button "SoundOff". Name the sound-on-button "SoundOn".

❑ If you have time you can experiment with adding an over and a down state for the buttons.

❑ Import a small sound loop into Flash.

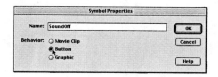

What is a sound loop? This is not a great explanation but hopefully it will help. The melody (not the words) for Row Row Row your Boat could make a small sound loop. After 20-some notes the melody repeats. All we need is that 20-some notes and we let Flash provide the repeat for us.

The Project

Rather than placing the sound in the Flash movie, we will leave it in the library. In order to control a sound that is in the library we need to set its "Linkage", which basically means to give it a name and to tell Flash that it can be used from the library.

❏ Select the sound in the Library palette, then choose the Options pop-out menu and select Linkages.

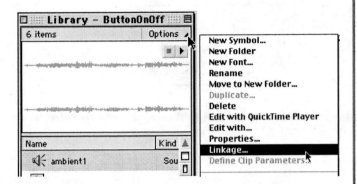

The Identifier is how ActionScript will refer to the sound, so choose a name that you will be able to remember later.

❏ Use the Identifier "music" for this sound, as shown. Set the Linkage to "Export this Symbol", then close this dialog.

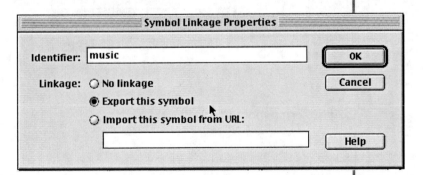

CREATING THE SOUNDOFF BEHAVIOR

Adding the ActionScript:

❏ Select the off-button, on the stage, then choose the Edit Actions button from the Instance palette, as shown. This should display the Object Actions window.

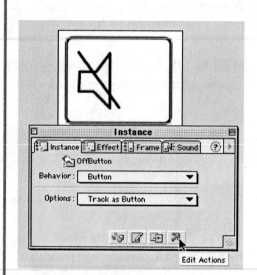

❏ Select the plus(+)-Basic Actions-Stop All Sounds command from the pop-out menu.

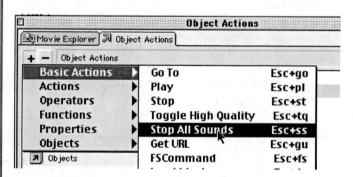

THE STOP SOUND SCRIPT

❏ The script should look like the following.

```
on (release) {
  stopAllSounds ();
}
```

❏ Close the Object Actions dialog. The sound-off-button is now complete.

For the on-button the scripting is a little more involved.

❑ Select the on-button, on the stage.

❑ Choose the Edit Actions on the Instance palette to open the Object Actions for the on-button. (see diagram)

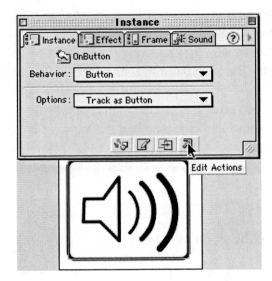

❑ In the upper right corner of Object Actions window is a pop-out menu. Select it and select Expert Mode. This will allow you to type code directly into Flash.

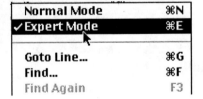

❑ Type in the following code exactly as shown.

```
on (release) {
  mySound = new Sound();
  mySound.attachSound("music");
  mySound.start(0, 50);
}
```

**ACTIONSCRIPT TO PLAY
LINKED LIBRARY SOUND**

DISSECTING THE CODE

```
on (release) {
  mySound = new Sound();
  mySound.attachSound("music");
  mySound.start(0, 50);
}
```

DEBUGGING: CATCHING CODE ERRORS

Explantation of the code:

On release is the event that triggers the following actions.

`mySound = newSound();` creates a variable mySound as a container that can hold sound.

`mySound.attachSound("music");` attaches the linked library file to the variable mySound.

Note: that the name we used in the Symbol Linkage properties (for the library sound) must exactly match the name used in the attachSound command.

`mySound.start(0,50);` starts the sound playing and uses the loop parameter to repeat it for 50 times.

To summarize. A variable is created, "mySound" the sound is attached to the variable, then the variable is told to play and loop.

Checking for Errors:

❏ 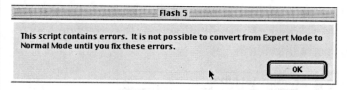 Change the scripting mode from Expert back to Normal.

If there are any major errors or omissions Flash will not allow you switch modes and will display an alert message.

Flash 5
This script contains errors. It is not possible to convert from Expert Mode to Normal Mode until you fix these errors.   OK

Flash will also display the Output dialog which will inform you what the problem is.

```
                                    Output
Generator Installed                                          Options
Scene=Scene 1, Layer=Layer 1, Frame=1: Line 2: Operator '=' must be followed by an operand
        mySound = new Sound(;

Scene=Scene 1, Layer=Layer 1, Frame=1: Line 3: ')' or ',' expected
        mySound.attachSound("music");
```

❑ Once you have corrected any major errors, and are able to switch back to the Normal Mode, you should see a script that looks like the following, without the error.

Error Note: The following code is correct except for the period (.) in the second line of code. Flash highlights the error and provides a description of the error at the bottom of the window. The error can be edited using the Value field at the bottom of the actions window.

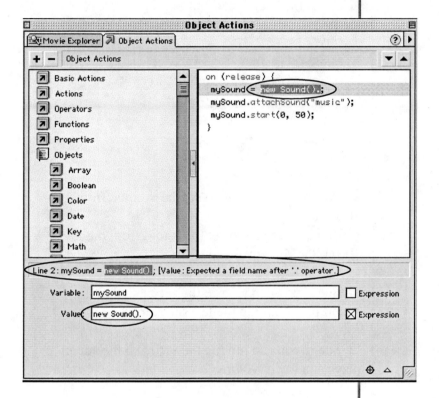

❑ Close Object Actions and test the movie. Note the sound will not start until you click on the start button.

❑ Save and publish this file as an .SWF.

POSSIBLE SCRIPT ERRORS

There are two areas where a problem might occur yet Flash would not see it as an error. Not spelling the Variable consistently and not spelling your linkage name correctly. If for some reason this script does not work then check those two items first.

ADDITIONAL EXPERIMENTATION

Additional Exploration.

1. See if you can find a way to get the sound to start when the movie starts. Hint: this does not require any scripting (timeline) although you could use ActionScript to have the sound start when the movie opens.

2. See if you can import another sound and use the same movie with a new sound.

3. The following shows two new lines of code added to the sound start button.

```
on (release) {
  mySound = new Sound( );
  mySound.attachSound("music");
  mySound.setVolume(100);
  mySound.setPan(-100);
  mySound.start(0, 50);
}
```

setVolume allows you to set the volume from 1 to 100 and
setPan allows you to set the sound from the left (-100)to the right (100) speaker.

❑ See if you can rewrite the script so that the sound plays only in the left speaker

❑ See if you can rewrite the script so the sound plays at a lower volume.

❑ Create three small buttons that fit onto the stage and allow the user to choose different sound volume of either, loud, medium and quiet. The script examples are shown to the left. The key to having these buttons work is using the same variable (mySound).
Once you get the buttons to work create simple graphic symbols that allow the user to visually understand the purpose of these sound volume buttons. Try to create the symbols without using text.

Loud Button
```
on (release) {
  mySound.setVolume(100);
}
```

Medium Button
```
on (release) {
  mySound.setVolume(60);
}
```

Quiet Button
```
on (release) {
  mySound.setVolume(40);
}
```

CHAPTER 19
Interactive MovieClips

This is where the real fun begins. Now that you know how to create an animation, a button symbol, and use basic ActionScript, the **movieclip** feature opens the door to power-user web creation.

A movieclip is an animation that is saved as a symbol. Clips allow you to combine several, if not hundreds, of short movies to create products that can be extremely complex and highly interactive. Hopefully, in this first example, you will be able to see some of the potential that is captivating Flash users.

As you explore this basic project, think about the different ways you can use these capabilities when creating your own web content.

For this project you will first create a simple animated button that stops when the user rolls over it, and starts when the user rolls off. The animated button will then be converted into a movieclip that can be used repeatedly in other animations. In the next chapter we will use the animated button clip from this chapter, to create an interactive Web game.

As you continue to work with Flash you'll want to refer to this chapter to review the steps on "converting an animation into a movieclip".

Topics

ADDING ACTION SCRIPT 114
SCRIPT VIEW 114
ADDING A SECOND EVENT SCRIPT 115
MODIFYING AN EVENT SCRIPT 115
SAVE THIS MOVIE 116
BUTTON INTO A MOVIECLIP 116
SELECTING ALL FRAMES 116
COPYING AN ANIMATION 116
CREATE A MOVIECLIP SYMBOL 117
PASTE FRAMES INTO A MOVIECLIP 117
USING THE MOVIECLIP 118
FURTHER EXPERIMENTATION 118

❑ Create a new movie that is 100 pixels high and 400 pixels wide.

❑ Create a circle on the stage and convert it into a button symbol called "ballButton." Add a simple over and down state to the button.

❑ In the lower left corner of the stage, set view to 25%.

❑ Place the button beyond the far left edge of the stage, as shown below.

❑ Insert a keyframe on frame 50, and then position the button beyond the far right edge of the stage.

❑ Create a motion tween so the button moves from the far left slowly beyond the right edge of the stage, see diagram.

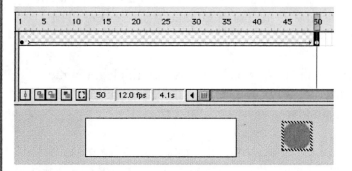

ADDING ACTION SCRIPT

❑ With frame 1 selected, choose Edit Actions from the Instance palette.

❑ Choose Basic Actions, and double click the Stop Action.

```
Basic Actions
    Go To          on (rollOver) {
    Play               stop ();
    Stop           }
```

❑ Select the first line of the script "on(Release)" and change the parameters to "on(Rollover) as shown. *The script you just created tells the player that when you roll over the button the movie should stop. To complete this project we want to add another script to resume play when the cursor rolls off of the button.*

❑ Select the last line in the script.

```
on (rollOver) {
  stop ();
}
```

❑ Double click Play from the Basic Actions.

```
Basic Actions    on (rollOver) {
    Go To            stop ();
                   }
    Play           on (release) {
                       play ();
                   }
```

❑ Select the new "on(release)" line and change the event to Roll Out (see diagram at right).
Your Script should now look like the following...

```
on (rollOver) {
  stop ();
}
on (rollOut) {
  play ();
}
```

❑ Test this movie using the Control-TestMovie command.

MODIFYING AN EVENT SCRIPT

```
Event: ☐ Press              ☒ Roll Over
       ☐ Release            ☐ Roll Out
       ☐ Release Outside    ☐ Drag Over
       ☐ Key Press: [      ] ☐ Drag Out
```

ADDING A SECOND EVENT SCRIPT TO THE BUTTON

```
Event: ☐ Press              ☐ Roll Over
       ☐ Release            ☒ Roll Out
       ☐ Release Outside    ☐ Drag Over
       ☐ Key Press: [      ] ☐ Drag Out
```

SAVE THIS MOVIE

□ IMPORTANT: Save this movie as "**buttonStop.fla**". We will use it for the next chapter to create a web game.

Note: **MouseEvent** scripts, such as "rollOver" and "press" can only be added to button symbols. Flash will not let you add a mouse event to either a graphic or movie symbol. On the other hand a button can be placed in a movieclip and the button will still act according to its script.

In the previous few pages you created a button symbol and added ActionScript to stop the movie when the mouse is over the button, and resume playing when the mouse was moved off the button.

Creating the Movieclip.

CONVERTING AN ANIMATION INTO A MOVIECLIP

□ Select all of the frames for this movie. To select all of the frames, there are a couple of approaches you can use. One is to click on any frame in the timeline then choose Edit-Select All. Another approach is to click on the layer icon.

STEP 1 SELECT ALL FRAMES IN THE MOVIE

If you had multiple layers your could also shift-click the layer icons.

□ With all of the frames selected, choose Edit-**CopyFrames**.
Note: there is a major difference between Edit-Copy and Edit-CopyFrames. Edit-CopyFrames will copy all of the selected frames in your animation.

□ With all of the frames copied, choose Insert-New Symbol.

STEP 2 COPY THE ANIMATION

Edit	View	Insert	Modi†
Undo			⌘Z
Redo			⌘Y
Cut			⌘X
Copy			⌘C
Paste			⌘V
Paste in Place			⇧⌘V
Clear			Delete
Duplicate			⌘D
Select All			⌘A
Deselect All			⇧⌘A
Cut Frames			⌥⌘X
Copy Frames			⌥⌘C
Paste Frames			⌥⌘V
Edit Symbols			⌘E
Edit Selected			
Edit All			
Preferences...			
Keyboard Shortcuts...			

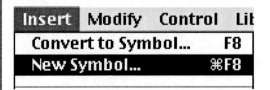

❑ Set the behavior to **Movie Clip** and name it "BallClip".

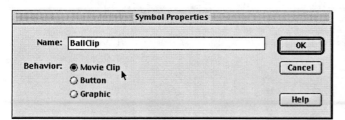

❑ When you choose OK in the Symbol Properties dialog (shown above), it may appear that nothing has changed. Look at the timeline and the stage, you will notice that both are empty indicating that you are in the symbol editor.

❑ In the symbol editor, click on frame 1 to highlight it, then choose Edit-**PasteFrames**.
*This will paste all of the frames of your movie into a single symbol (**movieclip**). This symbol can then be dropped into any new movie and will perform in the manner you created.*

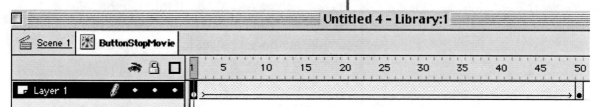

❑ Exit the symbol editor by clicking on the "Scene 1" button, shown in the diagram above.

❑ Open the Library palette.
Make sure the Library palette is displayed, and that you can see the "BallClip" displayed in the Library palette before continuing.

Creating a new movie for the movieclip.

❑ Choose File-New to create a new movie. Note that the library palette with "BallClip" is still visible in the new movie.

USING THE MOVIECLIP IN A NEW MOVIE

Here is how I have seen this effect used. A Flash animation has a cool background image, with movieclips floating across the browser window. When the user rolls over the clip it stops and the Over state displays text indicating that this is a link to another web site. When the user clicks on the button/clip they are taken to a different web site. This is accomplished by using the GetURL command in mouse press script in the button.

```
on (press) {
  getURL ("http://www.web.com");
}
```

FURTHER EXPLORATION

❑ In the new movie, drag several instances of the "BallClip" beyond the left edge of the stage. Place them at various locations, on the left edge. (See diagram.)
They can all be placed in frame 1 of layer 1.

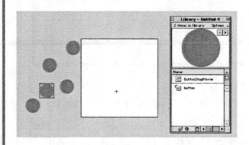

❑ Test the movie using Control-TestMovie. Is this great or what? Each object moves independently. When you roll over an object it only stops the individual movieclip while the rest continue to play.

Important: If you had problems with this project. I encourage you to walk back through the steps and try again. This is one of those concepts that can take a while but once you get it, you will be amazed at what you can do.

Further Exploration:

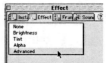

❑ Have each object appear in a different color or transparency. Select one instance of the BallClip on the stage, then experiment with the effects available in the Effect palette.

❑ If you have not already done so, change the Over and Down states of the buttons inside the movieclip. Note how the changes are reflected in all instances of the movieclip.

❑ See if you can create an animation where several animated movieclips link to a different web sites. See if you can figure out how to create a different over and down state for each separate movieclip.

CHAPTER 20

Interactive Web Game

This is a simple shoot-em-up web game that will extend your familiarity with movieclips. For this game you will modify the buttonStop movie created in the previous chapter. With a little imagination you will come up with a variety of objects that would lend themselves to the shoot-em-up game format. In addition, this project can also be used to create a variety of other interactive games. "Underwater Bursting Bubbles" is one example of a childrens game that is described at the end of this chapter in Further Exploration.

There are several components that make up a good shoot-em-up game. These are just a few.

1. A Compelling Idea. Something unusual, fun or creative to shoot at. Zombies are always fun, but instead let your imagination go wild. Come up with something amazing or bizarre.

2. Challenge. The object/s need to move and it should not be too easy to hit. Other challenge elements that are beyond the scope of this project are, scoring, and a timer. Both can be added, and will be discussed in a later chapter.

3. Sounds. Hey, what would a good shoot-em-up game be without the sound of a bang or an explosion when hit?

Topics

THE PROJECT 120
ADDING BUTTON STATES 120
OVER STATE GUN SITES 121
DOWN STATE EXPLOSION 121
ADDING THE BUTTON SOUND 122
EDITING ACTIONSCRIPT 123
MAKE THE BUTTON VANISH 123
CREATING THE MOVIECLIP 124
FURTHER EXPLORATION 125
USING THE MOVIECLIP 125
FURTHER EXPLORATION 126

THE PROJECT

In this project I am going to assume that you have read and understood the information in the previous chapters.

To produce this project you should know:

How to create and tween an object. Chapter 4.
How to create a button, and how to set it's Over, Down and Hit states. Chapter 12.
How to add sound to a button when the user clicks. Chapter 16.
How to access the ActionScript editor.
Chapter 12 -18.

Rather than start from scratch we'll use the file you created in the previous chapter called buttonstop.fla.

❏ Open the movie you created in the last chapter called "buttonStop.fla".

❏ Open the library palette, and double click on the button symbol. *If you cannot tell which object is the button symbol, expand the palette to see the labels.*

ADDING BUTTON STATES

❏ Add a keyframe to each of the states (if they are not already there.)

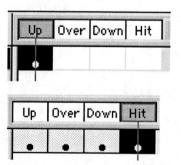

When the user drags over our button, we want to make it look like the button is in the sights of a gun.

This can be accomplished by changing the buttons color in the Over state. To access the button states, open the Library palette and double click on the "ballButton" symbol.

❑ To change the balls color: Open the button in the symbol editor, select the Over state, select the paint bucket tool from the tool palette, set the color to amber or orange and click on the button object to change its color.

❑ Adding the crosshairs: With the fill turned off, and the line thickness set to one pixel, draw a circle around the object. Then draw the cross hairs.

Now when the user rolls the cursor over the button, the user has the impression that the object is in the gun sight and ready for the shot.

❑ Select the button Down state. Use the lasso tool to select and break the button apart. The goal is to present the illusion that the object was shot. See diagram. If you want you can add in a bit of smoke and fire.

❑ To make the game more challenging you could make the Hit state smaller.
The Hit state does not show up in the animation but it does affect where the cursor must be placed in order to select the button.

OVER STATE GUN SIGHTS

DOWN STATE EXPLOSION

ADDING THE BUTTON SOUND

Now to add a gunshot sound. If you have a gunshot sound lying around, then do the following. If you do not have a gunshot sound choose Window-Common Libraries-Sounds and use the "Bucket Hit" sound. This sound is not ideal but will work for this project.

❑ Add a new layer to the button states.

❑ Select the Down state on the new layer.

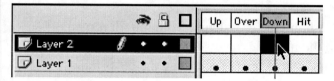

❑ Import a sound file. AIF or .WAV. (or use the Bucket Hit sound from common libraries).

❑ With the down state selected, drag the sound onto the stage.

❑ Return to <u>Scene 1</u>.

❑ Choose Control-Test Movie to see how it works so far. When you roll over the button it appears in the crosshairs of the gun. When you successfully click on the moving button, the gun fires.

There are still two problems with this game.

1. The button stops when the user rolls over it. *Kinda reduces the challenge of the game!*

2. After the button has been shot it explodes but then reappears and continues on its merry way. *"Hey, when I shoot a button I want it to vanish into the digital netherworld, not continue on as if nothing had happened!!"*

Both of these problems can be solved by changing the ActionScript for this button.

❑ Select frame 1 of the timeline, click once on the button on the stage, then select the Edit Actions button on the Instance palette .

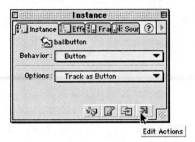

❑ Select and delete all of the scripting for this button. *You can do that by shift clicking on the text or by using the minus (-) button.*

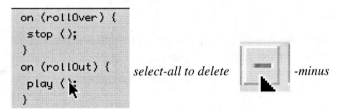

```
on (rollOver) {
  stop ();
}
on (rollOut) {
  play ();
}
```
select-all to delete   *-minus*

❑ In the actions window, select Properties and select _visible, see diagram at right.

❑ In the actions window double click on the _visible statement and add the following "_visible=false". See diagram below.

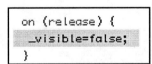

Expression: _visible=false

Your script should look like the following.

This script says that when the button is clicked it will vanish, or is no longer visible.

```
on (release) {
  _visible=false;
}
```

❑ Close Object Actions and save this movie as "GameSource.fla"

This is not the final game. It is the source file that will be used for the final game.

ACTIONSCRIPT TO MAKE THE BUTTON VANISH

CREATING THE MOVIECLIP

❑ Choose Control-Test Movie to see if the movie is working properly. When the user rolls over the button it should change in appearance. When the user successfully clicks on the button it should make a gun fire sound, explode, and vanish.

Now to create the final game. In order to have a truly exciting game we will need to have several instances of this object. *A game with only one target seems kinda boring.* With Flash and movieclips creating several instances is easy. In the next few steps you will convert this animation into a movieclip then place several instances on the stage of a new movie.

❑ Select all of the frames for this movie.
Either click on a frame in the time line, and choose Edit-Select all, or shift click on the layer icons to select all of the frames.

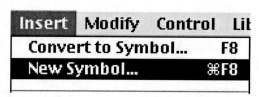

❑ Choose Edit-Copy**Frames**.

❑ With all of the frames copied choose Insert-New Symbol.

Insert	Modify	Control	Lil
Convert to Symbol...			**F8**
New Symbol...			**⌘F8**

❑ Select the movieclip option and name it "GameClip".

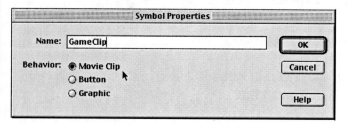

❏ In the symbol editor, click on frame 1 to select it, then choose Edit-Paste **Frames**.

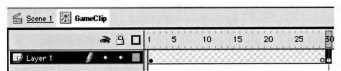

This will paste all of the frames of your movie into a single movieclip symbol .

❏ Open the Library palette.
Make sure the Library palette is displayed, and that you can see the GameClip before you continue on.

Creating the final game movie:

❏ Choose File-New to create a new movie. Set the size to 640 x 480, standard web page size. *Note the library palette with the movieclip is still visible in the new movie.*

❏ In the New Movie, drag 10-20 copies of the GameClip to the far left side off the stage. Stagger the placement. *They can all be placed in frame 1 of layer 1.*

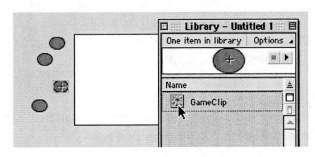

❏ Test the movie using Control-TestMovie.
You now have a Flash Game, with sound, animation, and a challenging target to shoot at.

FURTHER EXPLORATION

This is just the beginning of what can be produced using Flash and movieclips.

Further Exploration:
1. Come up with an interesting concept for a shoot-em-up game. Create the graphics, then follow the steps in this project to develop something new, unique and interesting.

2. Underwater Bursting Bubbles
The following is an example of how you can use the same project to create an interesting children's game that is non-violent but still utilizes the point and shoot techniques discussed here. (My daughter loves the little mermaid)

Create a graphic of a bubble using either Photoshop or Illustrator. Create a small movie, that is narrow but at least 480 pixels tall. Convert the bubble into a button that is animated to rise towards the top. Add a graphic to the down state of the bubblebutton that makes it appear to pop. Add a "pop" sound to the down state of the bubblebutton. Script the button to vanish when the user releases the mouse. Convert the single bubble animation into a movieclip. Create a new movie that is 640x480 with a background image of an underwater scene. Place 10-20 instances of the bubblePop clip at the bottom of the stage.

3. Experiment with some of the ideas discussed in the **"Project Notes:"** on the previous page.

4. If you can come up with some killer, cool, creative, interesting ideas for a web game, create it, and upload it to your web site, then email me with the web address. If I am impressed, or if it is incredibly unusual or experimental, I will post a link and mention you and it in the next edition of this book.

I look forward to seeing what you can come up with!!!

Reverse Engineering Flash Web Content

If you enjoy challenge, then think of this project as a quiz. If you are not a "quiz" kind of person then think of this project as an opportunity to learn how to reverse engineer some of the cool stuff that you have seen on the web. One of the things that I enjoy is seeing the stuff that others produce with Flash and trying to figure out how they did it. This project will take you step-by-step through the process of reverse engineering a Flash movie that was created using movieclips. As a Flash instructor, one of my concerns with producing a step-by-step book is insuring that the readers are actually learning Flash and not just learning how to follow my instructions. While this project is a departure from previous examples I hope you will enjoy it and also demonstrate to yourself how much you have learned about Flash.

This project is based on a Flash animation I ran across called "Green". When it opened, the browser window was solid black, and as I moved the cursor "squares of green" would light up and then slowly and gently fade out. I was dazzled and had to stop and play for a while. Because of the apparent complexity I assumed it was produced with Director and had a lot of involved scripting. I was really surprised to see that it was produced with Flash. (At the time Flash had minimal scripting.) It took me a while to realize what the author had done to create the effect. Since then, I have found a large number of very cool Flash sites that use the same basic concept in a variety of different ways.

FLASH QUIZ PROJECT

The original project was produced by an individual that I consider to be a Flash Guru. The question, then is, if you can figure out how to produce this project does that make you a "Flash Guru"? It is kind of like being Einstein and developing the theory of relativity, and those few experts who can actually understand it. Being able to figure out someone else's work puts you in the expert category. Being able to develop something new that everyone else wants to understand..., Hey, that, is when you achieve Guru-ness. If you have made it this far in this book, and have some creative ideas, I am expecting that you may soon achieve Guru status.

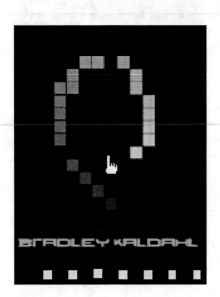

If you have problems with this project, do not fear, the next chapter will provide you with a step-by-step explanation of this concept, but I hope you will read through this project, and give it a try.

This project can be used in a couple of different ways. As a background for an animation, as an independent sequence in an animation, or as I have done, as a bit of eye candy and a pleasant surprise on a web page. I have embedded some small examples of this animation on a couple of my web pages in areas where I knew the user would likely discover it. I frequently receive feedback, from those viewing my site, that they find it very cool and wonder how it was produced.

Movieclips provide a way to create independant timelines. This project is based on the fact that Flash can have multiple independent timelines within a single animation. The two previous projects demonstrate this fact. A movieclip has its own independent timeline and can be placed in another movie which has a separate timeline. This project actually turns out to be fairly easy once you understand and feel comfortable with movieclips.

With this book, but especially this section on movieclips, I encourage you to think beyond the scope of the project. There is an amazing depth and complexity that can be achieved by using movieclips. I will not focus on steps with this project but instead the concepts. Hopefully, by this point, you are becoming more comfortable with Flash. On the other hand, do not despair if this particular concept does not come quickly. This is one of those projects that will continue to make more and more sense and reveal new possibilities over time. Even as I write this text I find new and different ways that this concept can be used.

What is the concept to which I refer? It is, using buttons inside movieclips to control the playback and behavior of the animation inside the movieclip. WOW!

So pump up your neurons and get prepared for some really cool stuff.

About the project:

You will create a Flash animation that starts out as a black screen and when the user rolls over the animation, squares of yellow will flash to life then gradually fade out. The question is how can you create little squares, that light up, then gradually fade out? The answer is with movieclips, of course. Each tiny square is actually a separate tiny movieclip running on its own independent timeline.

Reverse Engineering Flash

When trying to reverse engineer other Flash sites it is better to think of the components used to create the final animation rather than focusing on the entire animation. Unravel the individual pieces that were used to create the whole. Once you have an idea of how one piece should act then experiment with creating the same effect.

Dissecting an Animation

For this project, you want to think about an animation that uses a single square that starts out as black, then changes to bright yellow when the user rolls over it with the mouse, and gradually fades back to black. To really understand this animation lets break it down into individual parts.

Picking Apart the Pieces

Can you imagine an animation where a square starts out as bright yellow then gradually fades into Black? Actually it's kind of simple when you think about it. Create a square that is bright yellow and convert it into a graphic symbol. Add a new keyframe later on the timeline and set the alpha of the yellow square to 0% (transparent). Then create a tween from the first frame (full color) and the final frame (transparent). This produces a square that starts as bright yellow, then gradually fades out over time.

Putting the Animation Pieces Together

OK so we unraveled the second half of the animation. We have a yellow square that gradually fades out. Now for the first half of the animation. It starts as black before going to bright yellow and fading out. Of course the answer is that we have a black square that is the same size as the yellow square.

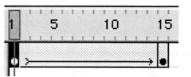

Frame 1

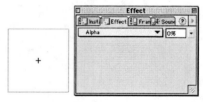

Frame 15

Putting it on a Flash Timeline

From frame 1-9 we have a black square. From frame 10- 25 the square appears as bright yellow then fades into nothing. Now that we have figured out how to create the basic animation the rest is simply a matter of adding some control.

Create an animation like the diagram shown above then choose Control-Test Movie to see how it works. At this point, the animation plays for several frames as a black square then plays for several frames as a yellow square that fades out, then loops back to the beginning to repeat the process.

Add ActionScript to Control the Movie

We need to add some simple controls to this movie to get it to stop before it reaches the yellow square, and wait for a mouse over event.

Step back for a moment and consider the ActionScript commands that could be used to make this work as intended. Before the user rolls over the black square, it remains black. As the user rolls over the square, it changes from black to bright yellow then fades.

If you think back to Chapter 14, dealing with stop and go animation, the answer is easy, when the animation reaches frame 9 of the black square, it stops and waits for user input. The way we get it to stop is using ActionScript on frame 9. Add a new scripting layer to this animation and at the end of the black square, on the timeline, have the animation stop.
See the diagram below.

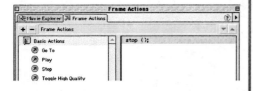

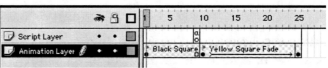

Frame action placed on frame 9 telling the movie to stop.
So now the animation stops at the black square and waits for user input.

Add ActionScript to Capture User Input

The next question is, how can we get Flash to capture user input? What type of symbol will respond to a mouse-rollOver event? The only symbol that will respond to a mouse event is a button. So, of course, the black square must be a button symbol.

Now that we know the black square must be a button, we can create it, and add an ActionScript to the button once it is placed on the stage.

The next question is what should the ActionScript say? Using the previous diagrams the button should have the following script...

```
on (rollOver) {
  gotoAndPlay (10);
}
```

Putting it all Together in a Movieclip

To summarize, we have just gone through the steps of creating a simple movie that starts as a black button, and waits for the user to roll over the button before it continues to play the rest of the animation. The rest of the animation consists of a yellow square that slowly fades to nothing. Because Flash automatically loops once the yellow square has faded out it will return to the beginning of the animation as a black button and again wait for user input.

The final step is to convert this simple animation into a movieclip. Once that is done, we can create a new animation that has a background set to black, and place a bunch of these movieclips into he new movie.

The next couple of pages provide the basic steps we have just discussed. Before reading the next couple of pages **test your knowledge.** See if you can create this project without using the step by step instructions. Reread the previous few pages. If you can produce this project based on the discussion of the previous few pages then you have arrived as a **Flash EXPERT**.

As an alternative, using a frame label, it could also say the following which is the same thing as the script shown above.

```
on (rollOver) {
  gotoAndPlay ("Yellow Square Fade");
}
```

FLASH EXPERT

The following instructions summarize this project:

• Create a new movie, set the size to 20x20 pixels.
• Create a yellow square that is about the same size as the stage.
• Convert the yellow square into a button symbol.
• Select the yellow square, on the stage, then select the Effect palette and set the brightness to -100% which will make it black.

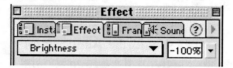

• Insert a Blank-keyframe at frame 10 on the timeline.
• Drag a copy of the yellow button symbol from the library palette onto the stage, and position it at exactly the same position as the black button square.
• Insert a keyframe at frame 25.
• Select frame 25 and using the effect palette set the alpha of the yellow square to 0%

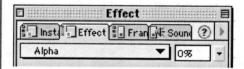

• Select frame 10 and create a tween between the yellow square and the transparent yellow square on frame 25.

Adding frame control

• Add a new layer to your animation and label it the scripting layer.
• Select frame 9 and insert a keyframe.
• Select frame 10 and insert a keyframe.
• Select frame 9 and double click on it to bring up the ActionScript dialog box.
• Create a Stop script.

Adding button control

• Select frame 1 of layer 1 and then click on the button on the stage to make sure it is selected, then choose the Instance palette, Edit Actions button.

• In the ActionScript dialog box, insert the script...

```
on (rollOver) {
  gotoAndPlay (10);
}
```

Creating the movieclip

• Select all of the frames of the animation.
• Choose Edit-Copy Frames.
• Choose Insert-New symbol and select movieclip.
• Select the first frame of the timeline, in the movieclip symbol editor, and choose Edit-Paste Frames.
• Test and save the animation before continuing.

Creating the final animation

• Open the library palette.
• Create a new movie that is 100 pixels by 100 pixels.
• Drag an instance of the MovieClip onto the upper left corner of the new movie.
• Continue to drag new instances of the MovieClip onto the stage and place them side by side.
• To help with positioning choose View-Grid-Edit Grid and set the grid size to 20x20 pixels.

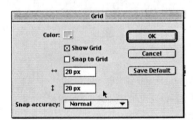

• Once you have several of the MovieClips in place and positioned properly you may want to use the Edit-Copy and Paste commands to reduce some of the tedious work of placing individual clips.

Older computers will slow down immensely using copy and paste but it is still much faster than individually placing 100 clips.
Remember to save frequently so if a mistake is made you can revert back to a previous version.

Final Note: If you were able to complete this project without referring to these step-by-step instructions then I am very impressed. Congratulations you have achieved a very complex understanding of this application. I would say that about 1 in 50 Flash users have the abilities that you demonstrate, or you have been working with Flash for a couple of years and have already become a Flash expert.

If you found you needed to use the step-by-step instructions in order to complete this project, you should feel proud, even if you found the step-by-step difficult to understand. The steps were not detailed and offered little in the way of illustration. You have come a long way and I'm sure that as you move forward you will be delighted with the deeper understanding that comes from continued experience with this application.

If you found that you were unable to complete this project, I would not be overly concerned. Instead look at the areas that caused you difficulty and review those sections and chapters. If you made it this far, and you are reading this statement, then obviously you have the tenacity and drive required to become a Flash expert. As an educator, it has always amazed me that often, those who spend the most time getting comfortable with a concept, are those who have the firmest grasp when all is said and done.

Move to the next chapter. It will take you step-by-step through a similar but also a very cool movieclip project that will further increase your understanding of this project.

A student showed me a very cool site from Sweden. The author was apparently a photographer as well as a Flash artist. As I entered the site, soft background music was playing and I was presented with a solid white page and a Title that stated that these were photographs of Sweden. As I moved the cursor over the white screen, it became a series of animated white objects that shrank, swirled, or faded out to display the image beneath. I love photography but basic landscape shots don't really intrigue me. On the other hand, I am so captivated by how this photographer incorporated a sense of exploration into the photographs using Flash that I revisit the site often.

Using this technique (or some variation) will not only enhance an image based site, but can also speed perceived user download time over slower connections because of the streaming capabilities in Flash, as well as traditional JPEG compression features.

The screen shots do not do justice to the experience of revealing a picture beneath. This is a project that a lot of my students have gotten excited about. After a lecture on this topic a student approached me and asked if the same effect could be produced using the image of worms or some such thing as opposed to simple white objects? The answer is

Topics

SCREEN SHOT EXAMPLE 135
PROJECT OVERVIEW 136
RELATED PROJECTS 136
CREATE THE BUTTON 137
PROJECT SETUP 137
CREATE THE TWEEN 137
CREATE FRAME CONTROL 138
ADD THE BUTTON CONTROL 139
CREATING THE MOVIECLIP 140
CREATING THE FINAL ANIMATION ... 140
ADDING THE MOVIECLIPS 141
FURTHER EXPLORATION 142

SCREEN SHOT EXAMPLE

RELATED PROJECTS

PROJECT OVERVIEW

yes but I still wonder, to this day, what creation that student came up with. I imagine one day encountering a web page that is covered with slithering worms and as you drag over them the image behind is revealed.

In a previous chapter, you produced an animated interactive web game using movieclips. What if the movieclips did not move but instead waited for the user to click or, roll over them? Then let's say that you create a new movie with an interesting photograph in the background. Rather than immediately presenting the photograph, you cover it with these animated movie-clip-buttons and, as the user drags over them, they explode or vanish slowly revealing the image behind.

As you explore the wealth of artistic Flash web sites, you will see that this concept is used repeatedly in a variety of interesting and unusual ways. As I mentioned, in first chapter of this book, this is the power user stuff that Flash offers. No other web publishing application that I know of, including Director, can provide this type of graphically fascinating effect. If you are a design artist, you will be absolutely amazed by the wealth of opportunities you have with this concept.

Project Concept

Just as in the previous project, you will create a movieclip and place several instances of it into a new final movie. The final destination movie will have two layers. Layer one for the background image and layer two for the movieclips which will cover the image until the user rolls over them.

The movieclip will start out as opaque white and respond to a rollover event by getting both smaller and more transparent until it has vanished. This project will take you step-by-step through the process of creating this animation but if you can figure out a Flash solution without using the step by step instructions, it will be to your benefit.

Here is the final movieclip timeline.

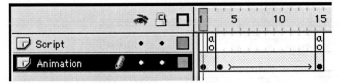

The animation layer has a white button that starts as opaque and stops on frame 2. Frame 3 - 15 tweens to transparent while getting smaller. The button instance on frames 1-2 has a control script.

```
on (rollOver) {
  gotoAndPlay (3);
}
```

The script layer has only two scripts. Frame 2 tells the movie to "stop" and frame 15 also tells the movie to stop.

Quick quiz: If frame 2 tells the movie to stop, then how is the user able to view the rest of this short movie?

Project setup

PROJECT SETUP

❑ Create a new movie, and set the stage size to 40x40 pixels. Set the background to black as this will help you to better see the white circle button you will create in the next step.

Creating the white button

CREATE THE BUTTON

❑ Create a white circle that covers the stage.
❑ Convert the white circle into a button symbol.

Creating the shrink and fade tween

❑ Insert a keyframe at frame 3 on the timeline.
❑ Insert a keyframe at frame 15 on the timeline.

❑ With frame 15 selected, choose the resize button on the tool palette and make the "white-circle-button" as small as possible.
Note: keep the circle positioned in the center of the stage. To help with centering, use the View-Grid-Edit Grid option and set the grid to 20 px x 20 px.

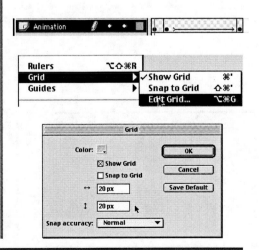

❑ With frame 15 still selected, use the effect palette set the buttons alpha to 0%

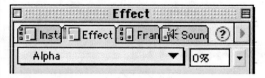

CREATE THE TWEEN

❑ Select frame 3 and create a motion tween between frame 3 and frame 15.

❑ Test the movie to see how it works.
The button should start as bright white then shrink and fade into nothing by the end of the animation. The next step is to add frame control to get it to stop while it is still white, and also to get it to stop at the end of the animation and prevent it from looping.

Adding Frame Control

CREATE FRAME CONTROL

❑ Add a new layer ⊞ to your animation and label it Script.

```
Script
Animation
```

❑ Select frame 2 and insert a keyframe.
❑ Select frame 3 and insert a keyframe.
❑ Select frame 2 and double click on it to bring up the Action Script dialog box.
❑ Create a "stop" script.

```
stop ();
```

❑ Select frame 15 and insert a keyframe, then double click on it to bring up the ActionScript dialog box and create a "stop" script.

```
stop ();
```

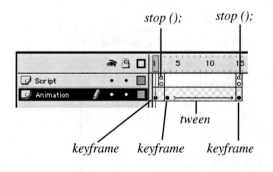

stop ();   *stop ();*

keyframe   keyframe   keyframe

tween

The timeline should now look like the example shown on the left.

With the frame control the movie will stop at frame 2, where the button is still large and opaque, and wait for user input. With the stop script on frame 15 we are assured the button will shrink, fade to transparent, and finally stop. We do not need user input on frame 15 because the movie instance is done.

Adding Button Control

❏ Select **frame 1** of layer 1, then click on the white-circle-button on the stage to make sure it is selected. Make sure you select frame 1. *(In order to apply actions to the button instance the Instance palette must display information on the button, as shown.)*

❏ Choose the Instance palette, Edit Actions button.

❏ In the ActionScript dialog box, double click the GoTo action. Modify the script to GoTo and play frame 3, as shown on the right.

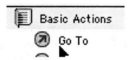

❏ Select the "on (release)" line of code and change the event to "on (rollover)". Your script should look like the example shown below.

```
on (rollOver) {
  gotoAndPlay (3);
}
```

❏ Test the movie to see how it works.
At start-up the white button appears unchanged, when the mouse rolls over the white button it begins to shrink and fade. If it does not respond in this way, then go back to the step on "Adding Frame Control" and walk through the steps to see if you can spot the error.

Trouble shooting tip: *If the button does not respond, the most likely cause is that the GoTo and play ActionScript was **not** applied to the button on frame 1. If this is the case, make sure you apply this action correctly then also find the mistaken location that this script was applied and delete it.*

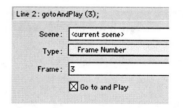

CREATING THE MOVIECLIP

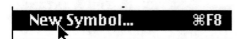

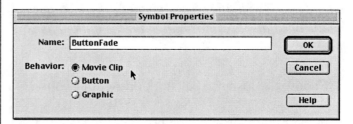

CREATING THE FINAL ANIMATION

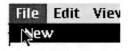

Creating the Movieclip

❑ Select all of the frames of the animation.
Click on any frame in the timeline then choose Edit-Select-all.

❑ Choose Edit-Copy Frames.

❑ Choose Insert-New Symbol.

❑ Set the symbol type to movieclip and name this clip "ButtonFade".

❑ Click on the first frame of the timeline in the movieclip symbol editor, and choose Edit-Paste Frames.

❑ Save this movie as "ButtonFadeSource.fla" just in case you experience problems.

You have now created a movieclip of this button and it's actions. This clip can be used repeatedly on a variety of images in the future without repeating all of the previous steps. To use this clip continue with the few remaining steps.

Creating the final animation

❑ With the "ButtonFadeSource.fla" movie displayed, open the library palette. Make sure that you can see the ButtonFade clip.

❑ Create a new movie that is 640 pixels by 480 pixels.

❑ In the new movie import a background image.
Flash prefers the PNG format but JPEG and GIF will also work. For this project do not worry about the image.

❏ Make sure the image is placed on layer one. *You do not need to add frames to this movie because the movieclip already has it's own independent timeline with all of the frames, actions, and animation required to make this effect work.*

❏ In the new movie, add a new layer.

❏ With frame 1 of the **new** layer selected drag a instance of the movieclip "buttonFade" onto the upper left corner of the new movie.

❏ Continue to drag new instances of the movieclip "buttonFade" onto the stage and place them side by side.
Trouble Shooting Note: If you are dragging instances of the movieclip and see small white dots, it does not mean you have been working too hard but instead, it means that there is a problem with the movieclip. Empty movieclips will show up as small dots. Walk back through the steps on "creating movieclips" to correct the problem.

❏ Test the movie to make sure it is working.

❏ To help with positioning choose View-Grid-Edit Grid and set the grid size to 20x20 pixels.

❏ Once you have several of the movieclips in place and positioned properly you may want to use the Edit-Copy & Paste commands to reduce some of the tedious work of placing individual clips. *Note: Older computers will slow down immensely using copy and paste, but it is still much faster than positioning individual movieclips.*

❏ Save and test.

I just love this effect!!

ADDING THE MOVIECLIPS

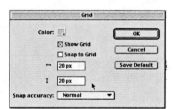

Empty movieclip

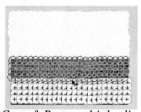

Copy & Paste multiple clips

Remember, you can use this clip repeatedly on a variety of different images. In addition, you can also open the symbol editor for the button and change its shape or replace it with an image to create a variety of effects. You can also open the movieclip and modify the rotation of the tween or the way it fades to add even more variation.

Further Exploration

Note: When you drag the movieclip onto the new movie, Flash copies both the clip and the associated button into the library of the final project.

Further exploration:
Open the Library palette, in you final project, and try the following to add more interest or diversity.

1. Double click on the white button symbol, in the library of the final project. Change the object from a circle to a square.

2. Double click on the movieclip symbol, and edit the tween (from frame 3-15) to spin while shrinking and fading.

3. Import a PNG-24 image to replace the button.
If you use a PNG image you will want to try to use an image that looks like it belongs. Worms, Rocks, grass, or anything that you might need to move to reveal what is underneath.

4. Edit the movieclip so instead of a motion tweened shrink and fade, you are using a shape tween from frames 3-15.
Remember a shape tween requires two objects that are not symbols.

5. What if the buttons faded-in before becoming solid? This would give the viewer a glimpse of the image beneath before they had a chance to drag over the buttons.

6. What if each button was a short animation that the user would drag over?

CHAPTER 23

Dynamic Text Fields

This project explores ActionScript and Flash. Generally variables are hidden inside the computer code and are never seen, but Flash has this cool feature that allows you to create a dynamic text field that acts as a variable. Part of the advantage of this is that we can see what the variable is doing. This can be helpful if you need to troubleshoot a problem script, or create a score counter for a game. Additionally this means you can use ActionScript to display and change text information directly on the stage or you can use ActionScript to capture user input, manipulate user input and store it for later use.

Note: if you are familiar with some of the older predecessors to Flash such as HyperCard and SuperCard, a dynamic text variable is analogous to a field. Flash has simply given an old dog a new name but when combined with Flash animation capabilities the possibilities are astounding.

Before jumping in, there is some terminology that will make this project more understandable.

Variables
A variable is programming jargon for a container that can hold information. Creating variables in Flash is relatively easy.
In the following example the variable "addStuff" is created and given a value of 10.

```
addStuff = 10;
```

In this next example the variable "myText" is created and holds the text Hello.

```
myText = "Hello";
```

Topics

IMPORTANT TERMINOLOGY BASICS 143
VARIABLES 144
NUMERIC VARIABLES 144
TEXT VARIABLES....................... 144
CREATING TEXT STRINGS 145
ACQUIRING PROGRAMMING SKILLS 145
THE LOOP COUNTER PROJECT: 146
CREATING DYNAMIC TEXT 146
ADDING A CONTROL LAYER 147
ADD A TIMER TO WEB GAME. 148
USING IF STATEMENTS 148

IMPORTANT TERMINOLOGY BASICS

VARIABLES

Variables can be given almost any name you choose, with the exception of reserved words used by flash such as "go to", "call", or "play". On the other hand you could use xplay or myPlay as a variable name without problem. It is also a good idea to give variables a name that helps you to remember what they do.

NUMERIC VARIABLES

Numbers

To provide a short example in Flash, we could create a variable called addStuff and give it a starting value of 10.

```
addStuff = 10;
```

If we asked for the value of addStuff it of course would be 10. If later in our animation, we created the statement

```
addStuff = 1+4;
```

addStuff would now have the value of 5. Note that 1+4 was NOT added to the value of 10 but instead replaced it. What if we wanted to add 4+1 to the existing value of addstuff. The script would look like the following...

```
addStuff = addStuff + 1+4;
```

Note: there are no quotes around numbers.

TEXT VARIABLES

Text

Variables can also contain letters or words. Most programming languages will refer to individual letters as **CHAR** (short for character). A bunch of letters strung together are referred to as a **string**.

```
textStuff = "a string of letters";
```

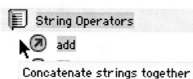

To combine letters to create a word or to combine words to create a sentence, or paragraph is referred to as **concatenate** which means to combine or to join together. In Flash a char or string will be enclosed in "quotes".

In Flash the concatenate operator is **add.**
In the example on the left, when button one is pressed, it places the chars "abc" into the variable called textStuff. When button two is pressed it adds the chars "def" to form a final string of "abcdef".

Button 1

```
on (press) {
  textStuff = "abc";
}
```

Button 2

```
on (press) {
  textStuff = textStuff add "def";
}
```

If a programming statement is used to join several different words and put them into a variable called **greeting**, it could look like the following...

```
on (press) {
    greeting = "Hi,"add" how"add" are"add" you?"
}
```

The result, would look like the following...

```
Hi, how are you?
```

To use programming jargon you would say that the first **char** of the first **string** in the **concatenation** above is a capitol H.
It would be silly to concatenate each individual word when instead you could simply create the variable called greeting using the following.

```
greeting="Hi, how are you?"
```

On the other hand you may have captured the user's name and stored it in a variable called userName. In order to concatenate the user name with the string, you might do something like the following.

```
on (press) {
  greeting = "Hi," add userName add " how are you?";
}
```

Note that in the above statement the string literals are enclosed by quotation marks but the variable that contains the users name is not in quotes.

If the information in this chapter does not make sense at first reading, take some time to reread it. It will help with understanding the following project.

One of the things that is enjoyable about applications like Flash and Director is that you do not need to be a programming expert, yet both applications offer easy entry into the world of computer programming. The concepts you learn here will be applicable to other programming languages, and by gaining some basic programming skills, you can dramatically expand the range of what is possible with Flash.

ACQUIRING PROGRAMMING SKILLS

THE LOOP COUNTER PROJECT:

CREATING DYNAMIC TEXT

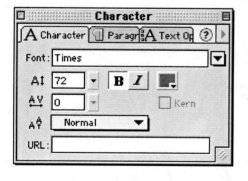

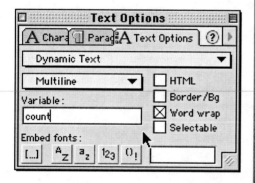

For this project we will create a variable that counts the number of times our animation loops and we will use the dynamic text feature to display this information on the stage.

❑ Create a new Flash document and make sure the background color is white.

❑ Using the text tool draw a text box in the center of the stage.

❑ While the text field is still active choose the Text Options palette. *Note if the text field becomes deselected it vanishes, simply draw a new text field.*

❑ Set the text options as shown. Choose dynamic text, multiline, turn word wrap on and selectable off. Most importantly name the variable "count." *The variable name can be any word you want. The key is to choose something that is both easy to remember and that helps to remind you what this variable does. Since this variable will be used to count the number of times our animation loops "count" is a good name.*

❑ With the text field still selected, choose the Character palette. Select a commonly used font, and give it a large point size.

Note: The text field relies on the fonts in the users computer. If you choose an unusual font, it will most likely revert to the users default of Times or Ariel. The text options palette does provide the option of imbedding Postscript font outlines in the Flash document but use this feature sparingly in order to avoid excessively large Flash animations.

Now that the text is defined as Dynamic Text, the text field will appear on the stage as a dotted outline. The dotted outline will vanish when viewed in a browser.

❑ Insert a keyframe on frame 10 of the timeline.

Note: Layer 1 contains the text field. Add a new layer to use for ActionScripting.

❑ Create a new layer.

❑ Insert a keyframe on frame 10 of the layer 2.

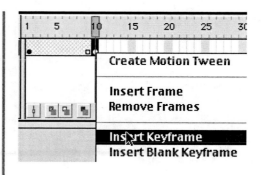

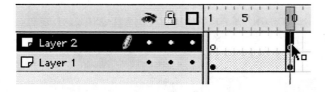

❑ Double click on frame 10 of layer 2 to display the ActionScript editor.

❑ Choose the "set variable" command from Actions menu.

❑ In the "Variable:" field, at the bottom of the Frame Actions window, enter the name of the text field variable: count.

❑ In the "Value:" area select the Expression button, then type in the Value: count + 1.

❑ The script window should display the following

```
count = count+1;
```

❑ Test the movie to make sure it works.

If all is working properly you should see the text field increment by one for every loop the animation makes. One way you might use this simple script is as a timer in an interactive web game.

If this where a timer for a game, then it might need an If statement to check the number of loops. After a specific number of loops it could go to another section of the movie that tells the user the game is over and display the game score.

Adding a Control Layer

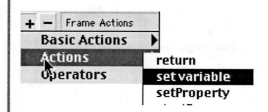

Designer Note: One way to use this bit of code is to convert it into a movie clip. Place several copies of the clip at different sizes against a futuristic background. Animate the clips and have them appear at different times in different locations. Apply some tint, or alpha effects to the individual clips and the final product is incredible.

USING IF STATEMENTS

goto	Esc+go
if	Esc+if
ifFrameLoaded	Esc+il

Go To	Esc+go
Play	Esc+pl
Stop	Esc+st
Toggle High Quality	Esc+tq
Stop All Sounds	Esc+ss

*Pop Quiz Question: How could you create a timer that counts **down** rather than counting up?*

FURTHER EXPLORATION

ADD A TIMER TO YOUR WEB GAME PROJECT.

If you want to add an "If" statement to this script, to check the number of loops, do the following.

❑ Double-click on frame 10 of layer 2 to display your ActionScript.

❑ Select the "If" statement from the Actions pop-out menu.

❑ In the bottom of the ActionScript palette, type in the Condition: count>9.

```
count = count+1;
if (count>9) {
}
```

Condition: count>9

❑ With the if statement still selected, choose the Stop command from Basic Actions. Your script should look like the following:

```
count = count+1;
if (count>9) {
  stop ();
}
```

❑ Test the movie to see if the "If" statement is working.

Note: that you could have easily dropped in a GoTo statement in place of the "Stop" command.

Further Exploration:

1. Experiment with the designers notes on the previous page. Create a futuristic animation with animated counting numbers.

2. If you produced the Web Game in the previous chapter, open the final game file. Make the final game 10 frames long. Originally it was only one frame long, using movieclips. Add a second layer and place a text field on the stage. Set the text field up as a variable. Add a third layer and place a frame action at the last frame to count and stop this movie after a certain number of loops.

CHAPTER 24

Typing Text Animation

If you worked through the previous chapter then you had an opportunity to work with numerical variables. This chapter deals with text variables and explores the effect created by dropping individual characters into a dynamic text field one frame at a time. The effect produced is analogous to a slow typist keying in letters one at a time. Because I have kept the ActionScript very basic the typing will gradually slow down over time. If you are a programmer you should be able to easily see why this animation slows and figure out a way to prevent it. If you are not a programmer, don't worry, the fact that this animation slows down is not a big deal and might even enhance the experience.

As you explore this project I'm sure you will come up with a variety of interesting and unique uses. One option, discussed in the further exploration section, is to use this project to create random falling letters, similar to the effect seen in the movie The Matrix.

❑ Create a new Flash document 640 pixels wide and 800 pixels high and set the background color to black.

❑ Using the text tool [A] draw a text box that begins at the left edge and goes to the right edge of the stage.

Topics

THE PROJECT 149
SETTING UP THE TEXT FIELD 150
ADDING THE SCRIPTING LAYER 150
CREATING THE SCRIPT 151
COPY AND PASTE A SCRIPT 151
FURTHER EXPLORATION 152

THE PROJECT

SETTING UP THE TEXT FIELD

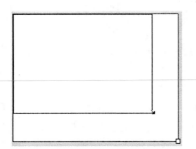

ADDING THE SCRIPTING LAYER

❏ While the text field is still active, choose the Text Options palette.

❏ Set the text options as shown. Choose dynamic text, multiline, turn word wrap on and selectable off.

❏ Name the text option variable "text".

❏ Now that the text is defined as dynamic, with the text tool active, stretch the text field so it covers the **entire** stage. Make sure the top of the text field does not go beyond the upper edge of the stage.

❏ With the text field still selected, choose the Character palette. Select Ariel, 48 point, and set the type color to bright green.

❏ Insert a keyframe on frame 6 of the timeline.

Adding an ActionScript layer

❏ Create a new layer.

❏ Create a blank keyframe in each of the six frames. *(F7 - or - Insert-Blank Keyframe)*

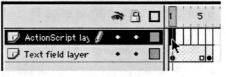

❏ Double click on frame 1 of layer 2, to bring up the ActionScript window.

❏ Choose the Actions- set variable, from the ActionScript menu.

❑ Set the variable name to "text", which is the same name as the text field you created on the stage. Turn **on** the Expression button for Value: , and enter the following, **text add "H"**. (See example below.)

| Variable : | text | | ☐ Expression |
| Value : | text add "H" | | ☒ Expression |

❑ The script should now look like the following.

```
text = text add "H";
```

Save some time by copying and pasting the script.
❑ Reposition the ActionsScript dialog so you can see it and the timeline, as shown on the right.

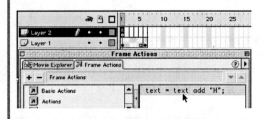

❑ Highlight the script. Either click, or drag on it, just as you would do if you were using a word processor and wanted to highlight and copy text. Once highlighted choose Edit-Copy.

COPY AND PASTE A SCRIPT

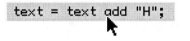

❑ Click on frame 2 of layer 2. You will notice that the script window in the ActionScript dialog goes blank. Click in the script window, then choose Edit-Paste.

❑ Edit the script of frame 2, by changing the letter "H" to "E".

❑ Click on frame 3 of layer 2.
In the Frame Actions dialog, choose Edit-Paste.
Edit the Script by changing the letter "H" to "L".

❑ Click on frame 4 of layer 2.
Paste the Script then replace the letter "H" with the letter "P".

❑ Double Click on frame 5 of layer 2.
Paste the Script then replace the letter "H" with the "!".

❑ Click on frame 6 of layer 2.
Paste the Script then replace the letter "H" with an empty space " ". Note that the blank space must be enclosed by quotes.

Not working? Check to make sure the text field variable name and the variable name you used in the ActionScript are identical. Also make sure the variable value expression button is on.

FURTHER EXPLORATION

Understanding the Script:
```
x = random(2);
text = x add "\n" add  text;
```

x=random(2); x is the variable, and random(2) will produce the random number of either 0 or 1.

text = x add "\n" add text; - In this line we are setting the text field so the new number will appear at the top of the field pushing all of the other numbers lower to create the letter falling effect. The "\n" forces Flash to add a hard return or "newline" after each letter.

Programmer Challenge: Log onto hotFlashBook.com and download the most recent version of the "Matrix.fla" to see a faster version of the code. If you can come up with a substantially faster implementation I will gladly credit you on the site and also acknowledge you in the next printing of this text.

❑ Test the movie to see if it works.
You should see the letters H, then E, then L, P, !, space, then repeat over.

Further Exploration:
Convert this movie into movieclip, call it TypingTextClip.

1. Use the TypingTextClip in a new animation. Have it start small then slowly expand in size. It will continue to type while it grows in size.

The Matrix:
The following example uses the same technique discussed in this chapter to create the Falling Letters effect seen in the movie The Matrix.
You can experiment with the brief instructions below or go to my web site, listed in Chapter 1, and download the file to see the code below with enhancements.

The trick to creating a Matrix effect is to get the letters to appear to fall or cascade down.
Create a text field that is about 2 characters wide. See the example on the left. *The width will be based on the font and point size that you use.*

Your timeline should look like the diagram shown at the left, frames 1-5 have the following script.

```
x = random(2);
text = x add "\n" add  text;
```

Frame 6 says go to frame 1 and play.
Once you get the letters falling, save this animation as a movieclip and place several of them in a new movie. NOTE: Too many copies of the movieclip placed onto a page will make the effect run slow.

There are some better ways to get this code to run faster. If you log onto the web site for this book you will get the most up-to-date, fastest code for producing the Matrix effect.
http://hotFlashBook.com

Flash Preloading

Flash provides streaming capabilities, which means that while your user is watching the first part of your Flash animation, the second part may be still downloading in the background. This is obviously a better solution than to make the user wait until all of your movie is downloaded before starting. If your Flash project is well designed, even users with a slow modem can begin to see animation while the rest of your content downloads.

What is a preloader?
In order to avoid long waits with content heavy movies, the author creates a small movie that plays and loops while the rest of the movie files are being downloaded. Of course the preloader should be as visually stimulating as possible, and it should be a prelude to the larger movie file that is being down-loaded.

This project will demonstrate a simple preloader script that will allow the opening scene to continue to loop while larger files continue to download.

What to include in a preloader: Simple vector graphics used as symbols, simple type used as symbols. Use only a few symbols to keep the file size small or introduce new symbols at later frames rather than on the first frame.
What you should not include: Large sound files, Scanned or bitmapped images, and by all means avoid using the word "Wait" as in please wait, or "Loading". Telling the user that they are waiting defeats the purpose of streaming content. If I know I am waiting then by nature I feel impatient, and annoyed that I have to wait. Rather than asking the user to wait, entertain them.

Topics

STREAMING MEDIA 153
WHAT IS A PRELOAD MOVIE 153
WHAT TO INCLUDE 153
THE PROJECT 154
Q&A ABOUT PRELOADERS 156
FURTHER EXPERIMENTATION 156

STREAMING MEDIA

WHAT IS A PRELOAD MOVIE

WHAT TO INCLUDE IN A PRELOADER

The Project

Project:

This chapter will be more explanation and instructions than a project. The following steps are provided for reference.

• Create a new Flash animation.

• Import a large movieclip, sound file, or scanned bitmapped image and place it into a new blank keyframe on frame 110. The large files on frame 110 will take a while to download.

• Create an animation from frames 1-100. This will represent our preloader so it should not contain any large bitmapped images, sound files, or video clips. If it is an animation, it should be designed to look acceptable when it loops back to frame 1.

In addition to a simple looping animation, you could also use the Interactive Web Game, chapter 20, Dynamic Text Fields, chapter 23 or the Animated Typist, chapter 24, as a preloader. The advantage with these three projects is that they require little or no download time, so your users get visual information right away. Of course, what you use as a preloader will depend on the audience you expect to see on your site.

The example below shows how the timeline might look.

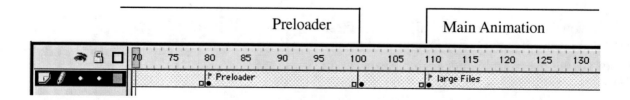

• Create a new layer for ActionScript commands.

• In frame 100, of the ActionScript layer, insert the action, shown below.
```
gotoAndPlay (1);
```

• In frame 99, of the ActionScript layer, insert the following ActionScript.

```
ifFrameLoaded (110) {
  gotoAndPlay (110);
}
```

The final timeline will look something like the example shown below.

When the playback head reaches frame 99 it will check to see if frame 110 is downloaded and ready. If it is ready the playback head will jump to frame 110 and will not loop back to the beginning. If frame 110 is not ready, then the playback head will continiue to frame 100 which tells it to go back to frame 1 and play the preload loop again.

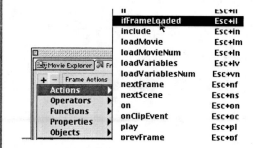

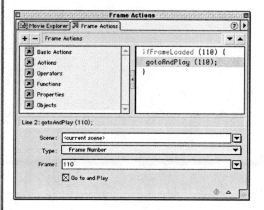

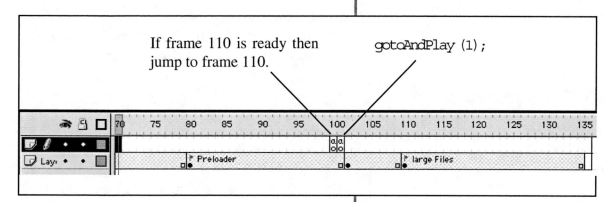

If frame 110 is ready then jump to frame 110.

gotoAndPlay (1);

The preloader is now ready. Even users with very slow connections will be greated immediately with your preload movie which will continiue to loop until all of the files have been downloaded. This technique could also be used to selectivly download portions of your movie while looping on selected portions. Users with a fast connection will never know the loops are there, but users with slow connections will be impressed with immediate and

Flash Preloading

Q&A ABOUT PRELOADERS

constant information. The next chapter will discuss how to test your preload clip to make sure it is working.

Commonly asked questions:
"After completing a large and complex movie I now realize I need to place a preloader at the beginning. How can I move the frames back to insert a preloader without upsetting the movie?"
Answer: Convert the large movie into a movieclip and place it in a new movie behind the preloader. You might even want to save your preloader as a movieclip for future use.

Another question is,
"what if I want the movie to jump out of the preloader and into the main movie as soon as the main movie is ready?"
Answer: While there might be more ellegant solutions a simple approach is to test to see if frame 110 is loaded every few frames.

```
ifFrameLoaded (110) {
   gotoAndPlay (110);
}
```
This solution will work but if your preloader is an animation then the animation will stop abruptly as the playback head jumps to your main movie.

FURTHER EXPLORATION

Further Exploration:
1. Convert the web game, from chapter 20, into a movieclip and use it as a preloader.

2. Rather than abruptly ending the web game, present the user with a button that allows them to continue. That way if the user is almost complete with the game they can finish before continuing into your web site. The diagram at the left presents an example of how this can be accomplished.

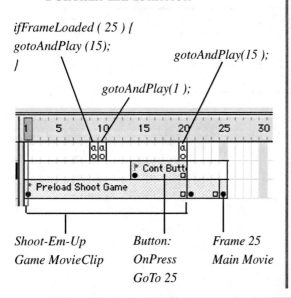

ifFrameLoaded (25) {
gotoAndPlay (15);
}

gotoAndPlay(1);

gotoAndPlay(15);

Shoot-Em-Up
Game MovieClip

Button:
OnPress
GoTo 25

Frame 25
Main Movie

Flash offers built-in capabilities to check your movie download speed with different types of connections. Flash not only offers the ability to see how the movie will playback but also can display, frame by frame problem areas or content heavy areas in your movie.

All of the testing takes place inside Flash by choosing Control-TestMovie.

This project is ideal for testing to see if your preloader is working and to determine how you users will experience your Flash site.

Topics

TESTING CONNECTION SPEEDS 157
PROJECT 158
MOVIE PLAYBACK OPTIONS 158

TESTING A FLASH MOVIE AT DIFFERENT CONNECTION SPEEDS

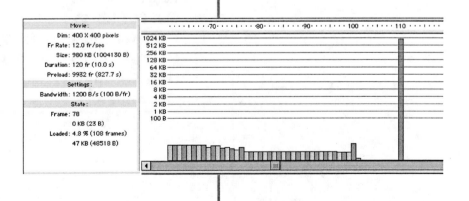

❑ Open a large Flash movie and choose Control-Test Movie

```
┌─────────────────────────────────────────────┐
│ Control  Libraries   Window    Help          │
├─────────────────────────────────────────────┤
│ Play                            Return       │
│ Rewind                       Option ⌘R       │
│                                              │
│ Step Forward                          >      │
│ Step Backward                         <      │
│                                              │
│ Test Movie                      ⌘Return      │
│ Test Scene               Option ⌘Return      │
└─────────────────────────────────────────────┘
```

❑ Once the Test Movie window finishes opening choose Control-Stop. Now that you are in the TEST MOVIE mode you can tinker with the different settings to see how your movie will play based on different connection types.

❑ Choose the Debug menu to select a download speed to test. Note that Flash allows you to create Custom-User Settings.

```
┌──────────────────────────────────────┐
│ Debug   Window    Help                │
├──────────────────────────────────────┤
│ List Objects                  ⌘L      │
│ List Variables               ⌥⌘V      │
│                                       │
│ ✓ 14.4 (1.2 KB/s)                     │
│   28.8 (2.3 KB/s)                     │
│   56K (4.7 KB/s)                      │
│   User Setting 4 (2.3 KB/s)           │
│   User Setting 5 (2.3 KB/s)           │
│   User Setting 6 (2.3 KB/s)           │
│   Customize...                        │
└──────────────────────────────────────┘
```

❑ Under the View menu turn on the Bandwidth Profiler, and the Frame By Frame Graph, then select Show Streaming.

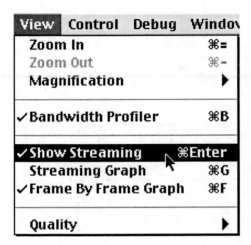

At the top of the graph a green bar represents how much information has been downloaded and is ready for playback. Additionally you can see the position of the playback head.

The Bandwidth Profiler, shown below, provides information about the movie. The area you are concerned with is at the bottom, which indicates how much of the movie has been loaded.

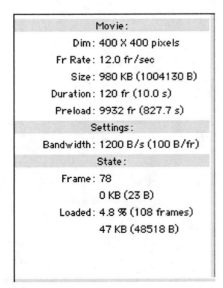

The Graph provides a frame-by-frame display of the download size of individual frames.

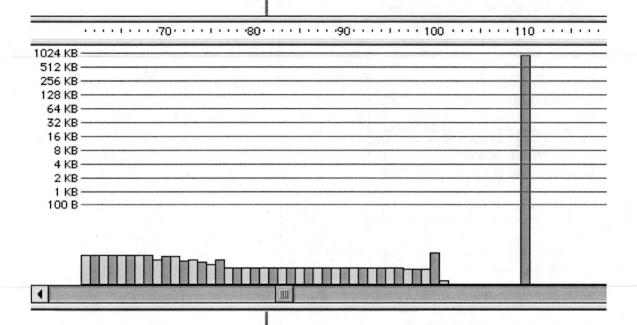

Additional Exploration:

Open a couple of your larger movies and experiment with different download speeds. Determine if there are any rough spots that might need adjusting.

Path Animation

CHAPTER 27

Path Based Animation

This is a relatively simple concept and can produce some great results. I saved it for a later section in this book because it is a buggy feature. The tutorial, and steps, included with Flash do not always work, for whatever reason. My teaching assistant came up with a procedure that may seem a little superstitious but it works 100% of the time. So if you have tried path based animation in the past and had problems, then this technique is worth trying. If you have never tried path based animation, you will have a good experience from the start if you follow the steps in this project.

What is path based Animation? Forcing the motion tweened object to follow a specific path that you create.

❑ Launch Flash and reset the palettes to the default layout.

Topics

THE PROJECT 161
WAIT ON THE TWEEN 162
PENCIL TOOL FOR GUIDE LAYER .. 163
APPLY TWEEN TO OBJECT LAYER . 163
ALIGN OBJECT TO MOTION PATH .. 164
ADDITIONAL EXPLORATION 165
SAVE AS A MOVIECLIP 165
PATH BASED SUMMARY 166

THE PROJECT

❏ Create a ball in the center of the stage and convert it into a graphic symbol.

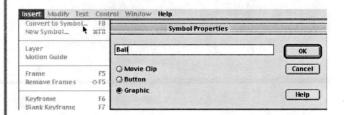

CREATE THE FRAMES BUT WAIT ON THE TWEEN

❏ Add a new keyframe at frame 30.

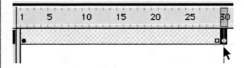

❏ Select Insert-Motion Guide from the menus. This will add a new layer to the timeline called the Guide layer.

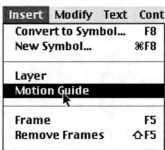

❏ Choose the pencil tool 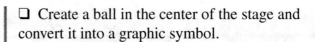 from the tool palette. You might wish to set the pencil tool options to "Smooth" but for this demo, it is not critical.

❏ Select frame 1 of the Guide layer.

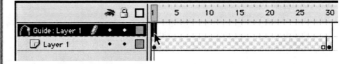

❑ With the pencil tool selected and frame 1 of the Guide layer selected, draw a path that represents the direction you want the ball to follow. Begin at the location of the ball and work outward. Try creating a spiral path as shown in the example. (Do not worry about making the path perfect, you can refine your technique later.)

USE THE PENCIL TOOL ON FRAME 1 OF THE GUIDE LAYER

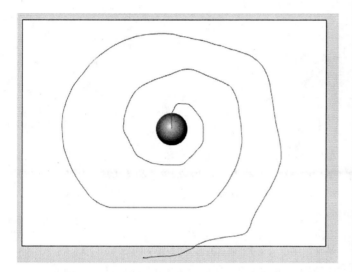

❑ Select frame 1 of layer 1.

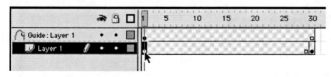

❑ With frame 1 selected, choose the Frame palette. Set the tween to motion and turn on the three options, orient to path, synchronize, and snap.

APPLY THE TWEEN TO OBJECT LAYER

ALIGN THE OBJECT TO THE MOTION PATH

❏ Select the last frame of layer 1. (As shown)

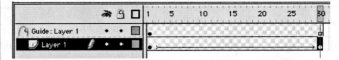

❏ With the last frame selected, move the ball so it's center point is on top of the ending point of the guide path, as shown below. If all went well you will see the object "snap to" the animation path.

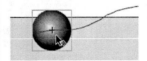

If the object did not snap to the animation path, or if you tested the animation and it did not follow the animation path then the following instructions should help.

❏ With the last keyframe of the object selected, set the Frame palette to motion tween, and turn on the snap option.

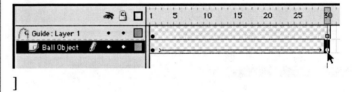

]

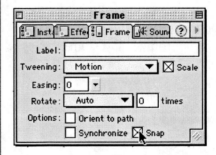

❏ Test the animation to make sure it works.

❑ Convert this animation into a MovieClip and call it "BallPathClip". It will be used in the next project, "Creating Onion Skin Trails". See examples below.

❑ Save this movie as "AnimationPath.fla".

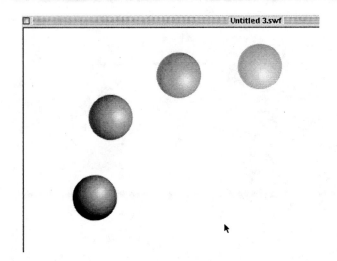

Untitled 3.swf

Additional Exploration:

1. Import an object from Illustrator or Photoshop and use path animation to move the object. The cool thing about path animation is that the object will rotate based on the path.

2. Create even more challenge with your web game. Open your web game Flash file and open the library. With the library displayed, create a new document. Follow the steps below to create a motion path for the animated ballClip. Remember, it is the center point crosshair that will follow the motion path. The center point crosshair for a movieclip may be in a much different location than the actual object that you see on the stage. See the diagram below.

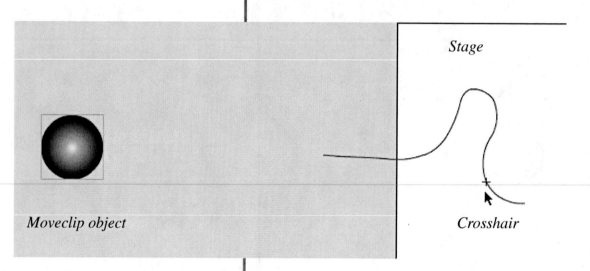

Stage

Moveclip object

Crosshair

Path Based Summary

The following is a summary of the steps in this project.

1. Place or create a graphic symbol on the stage, using frame 1 of the timeline.
2. Add a keyframe, in frame 3 or later, this is the ending keyframe.
3. Do not create the motion tween yet, instead choose Insert-Motion Guide from the menu.
4. Click on frame 1 of the **motion guide layer**, select the pencil tool, and draw the animation path.
5. Click on frame 1 of the object layer and create the motion tween. Use the tween options, orient to path, synchronize, and snap.
(You should see the object snap to the motion path.)
6. Click on the last keyframe, ending keyframe, of the object layer.
Align the objects center point to the end of the path or click on the last keyframe, select the motion tween and choose the snap option.

CHAPTER 28

Animated Motion Trails

Animated Motion Trails

If you have seen the movie The Matrix, there is a great trails effect . It appears that the actors are moving so fast that the camera can only capture the trails of their movement. When they stop the trails catch up. This project is an attempt to create a similar effect

One question I am frequently asked is...
"Is it possible to create the Onion Skin (Trails) effect in a Flash web animation?"
The answer is yes and no.
There is not a button, that can be turned on, to create the Onion Skin trails during web playback, but there is a technique that can be used to create the effect. The technique is easier than creating each and every frame individually, but it is not as easy as simply clicking the Onion Skin button. One positive feature of the effect is that as the animated object moves faster the trails become more spread out and when the object stops the trails will catch up.

To create this technique requires a knowledge of movieclips, and an animation that moves in some direction other than a straight line. The animation path in the previous chapter makes a nice fit for this project.

Topics

MOTION TRAILS 167
PROJECT 168
MULTIPLE MOVIECLIP COPIES 169

MOTION TRAILS

Project overview: The simplest way that I have found to create the trails effect is to use multiple copies of a single movieclip. Have each successive copy of the movieclip start 1-3 frames later than the original, and set the Alpha of each successive movieclip lighter than the previous. The diagram illustrates the concept.

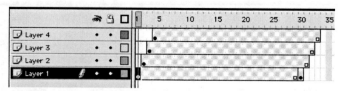

The step by step creation process is covered in the following short project.

❑ Create a new document and drop in an animated movieclip into frame 1, layer 1.
In the previous chapter you created the "BallPathClip" which will work well for this demo. Open the movie "AnimationPath" with the BallPathClip, and display the library palette. Create a new document. Drag a copy of the BallPathClip from the library palette onto the center of the stage of the new Untitled movie.

❑ If you are using the "BallPathClip" from the previous chapter then the original animation was 30 frames long, so add a keyframe on frame 30.

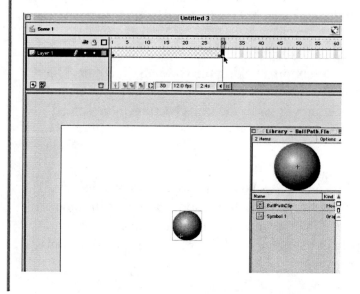

❑ Add a new layer to the animation.

❑ Place a keyframe at frame **3** of the new layer.

❑ With frame 3 still selected drag another copy of the movieclip onto the stage and position it at exactly the same location as the first movieclip.

❑ Set the **alpha of this new layer to 80%**.

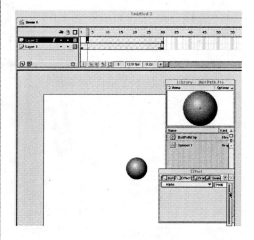

❑ Add a new layer to the animation.

❑ Place a keyframe at frame **5** of the new layer.

❑ With frame 5 still selected drag another copy of the movieclip onto the stage and position it at exactly the same location as the first movieclip.

❑ Set the **alpha of this new layer to 60%**.

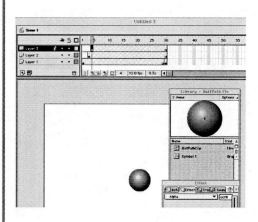

❑ Add a new layer to the animation.

❑ Place a keyframe at frame **7** of the new layer.

❑ With frame 7 still selected drag another copy of the movieclip onto the stage and position it at exactly the same location as the first movieclip.

❑ Set the **alpha of this new layer to 40%**.

❑ Test the movie to see the effect.

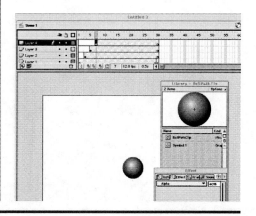

❑ To make the effect even more dramatic you could continue to add more layers, each with a lighter alpha than the previous layer.

How this effect Works: I am sure you have already figured this out but I will reiterate it in order to confirm your suspicions.

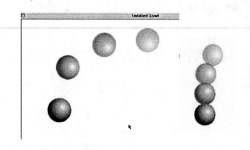

Each movieclip runs on its own independent timeline. By starting each copy of the movieclip 1-3 frames later it produces a duplicate animation that is a fraction of a second slower than the previous animation. By setting the alpha of each successive movieclip a little lighter than the previous clip it produces the illusion of trails.

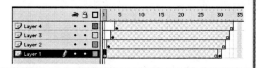

Pointers:
To make this effect really shine, each layer should have the same number of frames as the original movieclip. In the example shown, layers 2-4 were extended.

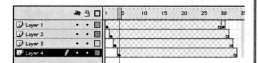

To make the effect look even better, the first layer should be on the Top (in Front of the other clips) and each successive layer should appear beneath.

This effect is really fun with an animation that moves quickly then pauses for a few frames then resumes fast animation. If you are familiar with the movie "The Matrix", imagine an animation that moves at high speed (the trails slowly follow the high speed movement) then the animation pauses for a moment. The trails will catch up with the original animation, and appear to pause. Then the animation resumes rapid movement which again leaves the trails to slowly follow. The net result is a surrealistic illusion of slow and fast movement which appears to be captured in slow motion.
You may also want to try this animation effect using, Chapter 8, Spinning Type, with the easing option turned on!!

CHAPTER 29

Collision Testing Score Keeping & Dragging Objects

Topics

PROJECT 171
DRAG OBJECT 172
IDEAS FOR DRAG OBJECTS 174
ANIMATING A DRAGABLE OBJECT .. 174
VARIATIONS ON THE SCRIPT 175
HIT TEST SCRIPT 176
KEEPING SCORE 176
FINAL SCRIPT 178
SCORE FIELD 179
HIT OBJECT 179
NAMING THE HIT OBJECT 180

This last Flash project will use a simple drag and drop game to cover three ActionScript issues. Making objects moveable, performing a hit test to see if one object strikes another and score keeping for a simple game. While the examples will be as simple as possible, these concepts are great for variety of interactive projects

❑ Launch Flash and reset the palettes.

❑ Create a simple ball on the stage and convert it into a button symbol.

PROJECT

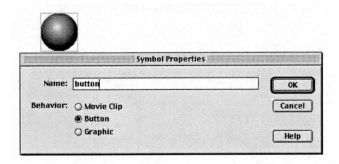

❑ Select the ball-button on the stage and display the ActionScript editor.

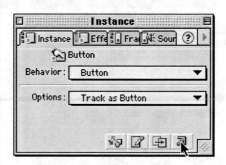

Letting the User Drag an Object

❑ Apply the startDrag action to the ball object, as shown. (Flash automatically adds the on release handler)

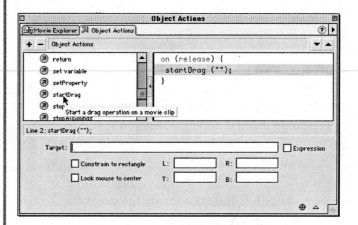

❑ Change on(release) to on(press) .

❑ In the upper left corner of the Actions window, select the pop-out menu to switch to expert mode.

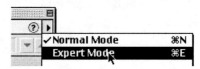

❑ Insert the word this. in front of the startDrag command. Make sure you include the period as shown.

```
on (press) {
    this.startDrag ("");
}
```

Now, when the user holds the mouse button down on the object it will move.

About the code. The term this. is great because we do not need to call the object by name. Instead Flash looks at the object that received the mouse press and applies the drag command to it.

❏ Change the Actions back to the Normal Mode.

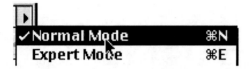

❏ Choose Control -Test Movie to see how it works.

When you click and drag on the object, it follows the cursor, but it never stops following the cursor. You might use this technique if you wanted to hide the traditional cursor and replace it with an object that you created to represent the cursor.

The following steps will show how to release the object when the mouse is released.

❏ Add the StopDrag command to your ball-button object as shown. (Again by default Flash places it in a on release handler for you.)

❏ Add releaseOutside to the event handler as shown.

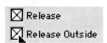

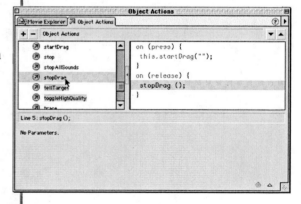

The drag script should now look like the following.

```
on (press) {
  this.startDrag("");
}
on (release, releaseOutside) {
  stopDrag ();
}
```

❏ Choose Control-Test Movie to see how it works.
The nice thing about this little script is that it is completely contained in the ball object. You could save this object as a movieclip and place hundreds

IDEAS FOR DRAG OBJECTS

ANIMATING A DRAGABLE OBJECT

of them in a movie and each object still knows how it should act.

One possible use for this script. Suppose your customer was a clothing retailer. Selling cloths on-line can be difficult because the customer wants to be able to try them on. One option would be to provide the user with a picture of a model and a variety of moveable shirts and pants.

Back to the project:

❑ To add interest, have the ball animate across the stage. To animate the ball, move the ball to the far left of the stage. Add a keyframe on frame 40. With frame 40 selected move the ball to the far right. Click on frame 1 and add a motion tween.

❑ Choose Control-Test Movie to see how it works. (It will not work as you might expect)

If the ball is animated and you attempt to drag it will not follow the cursor, but instead will change its animation path based on how you move it.

While this may not be what you expected it does offer some possibilities for interesting game ideas. The first thing that comes to my mind is a virtual bowling game, where the ball appears at a random area and begins to roll towards the end of the bowling alley. The pins, are in the center of the far end of the stage. The user must catch and align the ball in order to strike the pins.

For this project, what we want, is a ball that is both animated, and that the user can stop and drag around when they click on it.

Back to the ball-button script.

❑ Select frame 1 on the timeline, then click on the ball on the stage, then open the ActionScript dialog. (Make sure you are seeing Object Actions for the ball-button)

❑ Add the following lines of code to the ball-button.

```
on(rollOver) {
stop(); }
```

Note: This action is called on rollOver. This means the object will stop as soon as the user rolls over it.

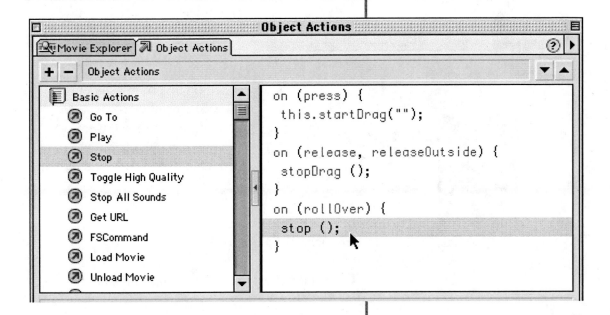

❑ Choose Control-Test Movie to see how it works.

❑ Save this movie as "balldrag.fla".

Note: Some variations on the Script
Placing the stop script in the on(press) handler will force the movie to stop only when the user clicks on the object. Additionally we could also add a play(); script to the release handler to have the object start moving again when the user is done dragging it.

The next part of this project will discuss hit testing and score keeping.

To understand the scripts that will be added you will need to know what the final project will do.

VARIATIONS ON THE SCRIPT

This is an example of a variation on the project script. While it is not what we want for this project, come back later to experiment with it.

```
on (press) {
stop ();
this.startDrag("");
}
on (release, releaseOutside) {
stopDrag ();
play ();
}
```

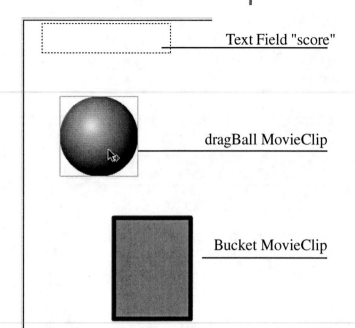

Text Field "score"

dragBall MovieClip

Bucket MovieClip

The final project will have several instances of the dragBall animation that we just created, saved as movieclip. It will also have a bucket that the user must drop the balls into. We will create a "hitTest" script to detect if the user was successful in dragging the ball into the bucket. Finally it will have a text field that will keep score of all of the balls the user drops into the bucket. Actually, this animation is based on one of my students idea. She wanted to create an animation where fish were floating through the air and the user would drag them into a fish tank.

HIT TEST SCRIPT

Summary of the ActionScript.

This is the hitTest code that is placed inside the dragBall object.

hitTest - Compares the location of two objects. If the two objects intersect then the hitTest is true.

```
if (this.hitTest(_root.bucket)) {
    _root.score += 1;
}
```

The hitTest begins with an *if ( ){ }* statement. **If** the statement in the parenthesis **()** is true then perform the actions in the curly brackets **{ }**.

(this.hitTest(_root.bucket)) compares to see if this. (the ballDrag object) hitTest (intersects with) the bucket in the main movie (_root.bucket) .

KEEPING SCORE

If the if statement is true then the following line of code is executed.

_root.score += 1; Add 1 to the parent (root) movie variable called score.

To restate the code on the previous page says if the ballDrag object hits the bucket then add 1 to the text field called Score.

Note: you could add a variety of additional actions to be executed when the ball hits the bucket. A sound could play to indicate the object was hit. The ball could disappear. You could also have either the ball or the bucket play a short movie, such as the bucket could jiggle or expand to indicate it is full.

Here is an idea, the ball could be set to disappear, then the bucket plays a short animation where it appears that the ball is grabbing onto the edge of the bucket struggling to stay out, before it finally drops down into the bucket!!
Well, maybe not, but you get the idea.

❑ Click on frame 1 of the ballDrag movie then click on the ball object on the stage and open the ActionScript editor. (You may need to set the ActionScript editor to expert mode to enter the code as shown.)

❑ Enter the following text after the on(release), handler. (See diagram)

```
on (release, releaseOutside) {
    if (this.hitTest(_root.bucket)) {
        _root.score += 1;
    }
    stopDrag ();
}
```

```
if(this.hitTest(_root.bucket)){
    _root.score += 1;
}
```

Make sure that there are two opening and two closing parenthesis (). Also, make sure there is an opening and closing Bracket { }for the *if* statement.

Your final dragBall script should look like the following...

FINAL SCRIPT

```
on (press) {
  this.startDrag("");
}
on (release, releaseOutside) {
  if (this.hitTest(_root.bucket)) {
  _root.score += 1;
  }
  stopDrag ();
}
on (rollOver) {
  stop ();
}
```

❑ Convert the ballDrag movie into a movieclip
To convert into a movieclip, click on the timeline, choose Edit-Select-All to select all of the frames of the movie. Choose Insert-New-Symbol and name the movieclip something like ballDragClip. When the symbol editor opens click on frame 1 then choose Edit-Paste-Frames.

❑ After creating the ballDrag movieclip, open the library palette.

❑ Choose File-New to create a new movie.

The new movie you will eventually have copies of the ballDragClip but first create the two objects that where referred to in our hitTest script. The hitTest script will look for an object, on the stage of the new movie, called "bucket". It will also need a text field variable called "score".

Creating and labeling the score text field.

❑ Select the text tool and create a text box in the new movie.

❑ With the text box still selected, choose the Text Options palette and convert the text field to dynamic text and enter the word "score" into the Variable field, see diagram.

Text Options

A Chara | Parag | A Text Options | ?

Dynamic Text ▼

Single Line ▼ | ☐ HTML
Variable: | ☐ Border/Bg
score
| ☐ Selectable
Embed fonts:
[...] | Az | az | 123 | () !

Creating and labeling the bucket clip.

❑ Add a new layer to the movie.

❑ Draw a simple square object on the stage to represent the bucket.

❑ Select the bucket object with the pointer tool, then choose Insert-Convert-to-Symbol.
Name it "bucket", see diagram and sure it is defined as a movieclip.

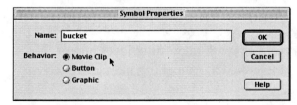

Symbol Properties

Name: bucket | OK

Behavior: ● Movie Clip | Cancel
○ Button
○ Graphic | Help

❑ With the bucket-clip object still selected, choose the instance palette and set it's Name: to "bucket". (all lower case) see the diagram.

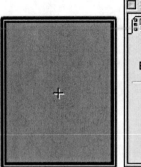
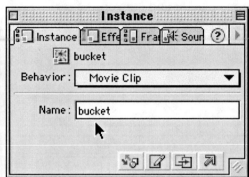

❑ Add a third layer to the movie.
Your timeline should now resemble the following diagram.

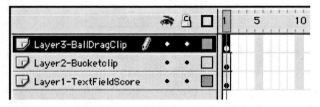

❑ With frame 1 of the new layer selected, drag several instances of the dragBallClip from the library palette and place them on the left side of the stage.

❑ Choose Control-Test Movie to see how it works.

Based on this simple project you have all of the tools for a variety of different interactive games. This project includes animated objects, being able to stop and move the object, detecting if the object hits another object, and score keeping.

As always this project provides the tools but it is up to you to come up with interesting ideas and exciting content to create a compelling interactive web animation.

Using Photoshop with Flash

Photoshop 6.0 type effects for Flash.

Photoshop and Illustrator are two popular applications for creating Flash content. This chapter and the next will demonstrate each of these applications. Illustrator creates vector content that is ideal for Flash. Photoshop is used for scanned or bitmapped image manipulation and provides a wealth of features and options that can be incorporated into Flash. Two additional applications that might be used with Flash are Freehand, which is the Macromedia vector based alternative to Illustrator and Fireworks, which is similar to Photoshop.

This chapter will focus on using and exporting a transparent image from Photoshop 6.0 for use in Flash. If you are using Photoshop 5.5 or earlier you should still be able to follow along without much difficulty. This is meant only as a brief introduction to Photoshop. This project will focus only on creating and saving transparent bitmapped type effects for use in Flash.

For those of you who know Photoshop, you may want to jump ahead to the Save-For-Web section of this project. For those of you who do not know Photoshop, take your time, and remember that Photoshop is vast. You will not learn this application in a single short tutorial. This project is only designed to provide an introduction to Photoshops

Topics

PHOTOSHOP 6.0 AND FLASH 181
THE PROJECT 182
SAVE FOR WEB 184
IMPORTING THE PNG INTO FLASH 185
MELTING HEAD.......................... 186

PHOTOSHOP 6.0 AND FLASH

export functions for use with Flash. If you find the features in Photoshop exciting you might wish to seek additional instruction.

The Project:

❏ Launch Photoshop 6.0

❏ Set-up.
In Photoshop choose Window-Reset Palette Locations

❏ Choose File-New

❏ Set up the New-Document dialog as shown.
Note: Make sure to set the background to Transparent.

THE PROJECT

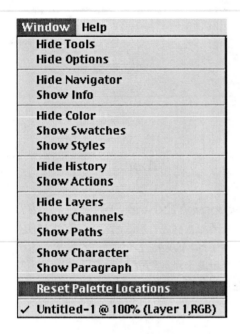

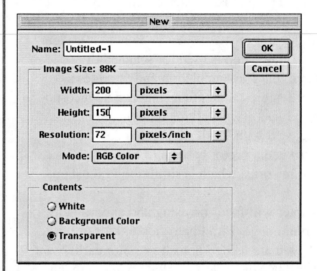

❏ Hit the D key on the keyboard to set the foreground color to Black.

❏ Select the Type T tool from the tool palette.

❏ Select the font and point size from the Options bar, as shown below. 72 points should work well.

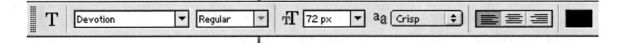

❑ Click in the image window with the Type tool, and type the word Flash.

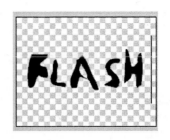

❑ Choose the pointer tool ![pointer tool icon] from the tool palette.

❑ Choose the menu Layer-Layer Style-Bevel and Emboss...

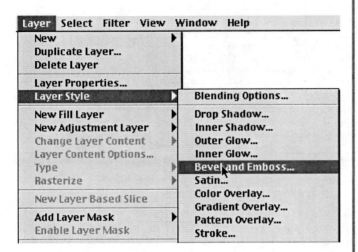

❑ Set the Style to Emboss. Turn on the Preview button. Experiment with the Emboss features until you achieve an effect that you like, then choose OK to apply the effect to your type.

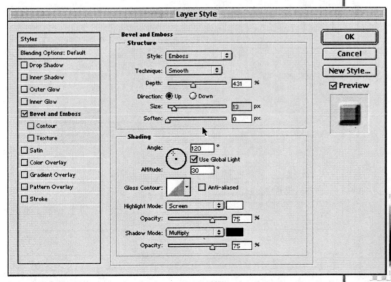

SAVE FOR WEB

Using the Save for Web menu command.

❏ Choose the menu File-Save for Web.

❏ In the Save For Web dialog select the PNG-24 option and make sure the transparency is turned on, then select the OK button.

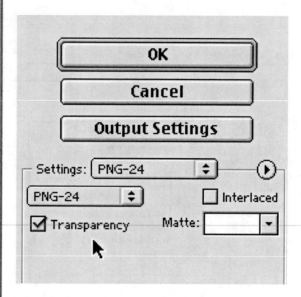

❏ Name the file and choose the location to save it.

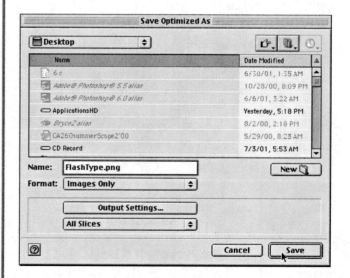

❏ Remember to use File-Save to save the original Photoshop file in case you need to make revisions.

❑ Launch Flash

❑ In Flash choose File-Import, and locate the PNG file you just saved.

❑ Select the file and choose the Add button. Note you can import multiple files if needed.

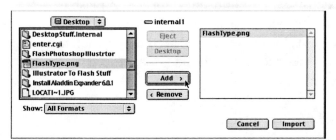

❑ When presented with the Fireworks PNG import settings dialog, choose OK to accept the defaults.

❑ The image will appear on the stage and also in your library palette for the movie.

Note how clean the edges of the transparency are when using the PNG format.

Imported PNG images will accept a motion tween, but they are still not yet considered a graphic symbol by Flash.

Extensive use of bitmapped images in Flash is perfectly acceptable, but you will want to perform download testing and may need to incorporate a preloader because of the additional file size created by bitmapped images.

Additional Experimentation:
1. Melting Head
If you are a Photoshop 6.0 user and have not yet discovered this feature be prepared. You are going to have a blast with the wonderful image distortions and effects you can create.

Open, scan or create an image in Photoshop then choose Image Liquify. Experiment with the setting and the distortions. Saving the distortions in small increments will work well with frame by frame animation.

ADDITIONAL EXPERIMENTATION
MELTING HEAD

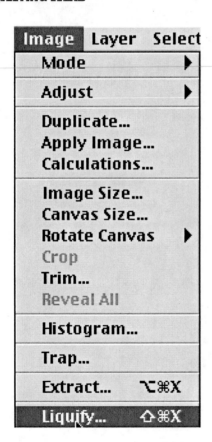

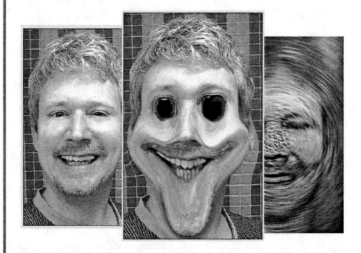

2. In addition you might want to experiment with some of the different filters found under the Filter menu.

CHAPTER 31

Using Illustrator with Flash

Using Illustrator 9.0 with Flash

This project will focus on how to export from Adobe Illustrator into Flash. Illustrator is a very robust application and, just as in the previous chapter, this project will not make you an Illustrator expert. It will provide additional options for creating images and artwork for use in Flash.

While Flash is an animation application that provides vector based drawing tools, Illustrator has been around for years and the primary purpose of this application is to produce vector art. While I have to admit that I am very impressed with some of the vector features in Flash, it is important to remember that it cannot, nor will it ever, do everything we might need. This project will focus on creating type on a simple path and exporting it as vector file for Flash. If you are a Photoshop 6.0 user you might be thinking that Photoshop can place type on a path and you are correct, but Illustrator offers much more control and has the huge added benefit of being able to export using vector as opposed to the bitmapped format.

If you know Illustrator you may wish to jump ahead to the section on export functions. If you do not know Illustrator, please remember, this project barely scratches the surface of this application. If you find the features in Illustrator exciting you may want to seek additional instruction.

Topics

ILLUSTRATOR 9 WITH FLASH 187
PROJECT 188
ILLUSTRATOR EXPORT OPTIONS 189
SWF FORMAT DIALOG 190
EXPORT OPTIONS 191
IMAGE OPTIONS 191
ILLUSTRATOR INTO FLASH 191
FURTHER EXPLORATION 192

USING ILLUSTRATOR 9 WITH FLASH

PROJECT

Creating type on a path for use in Flash.

❏ Launch Illustrator 9.0. (earlier versions of Illustrator do not have the export for Flash capabilities found in version 9.0.

❏ Create a new document in the RGB mode, with an artboard size of 4" x 4".

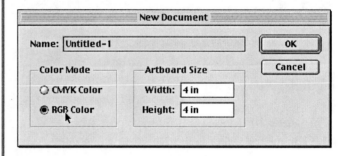

❏ On the tool palette, select the fill swatch and set it to none, then select the line swatch and set it to none (as shown in the diagram at the left).

❏ Select the oval tool and draw a circle in the image window.

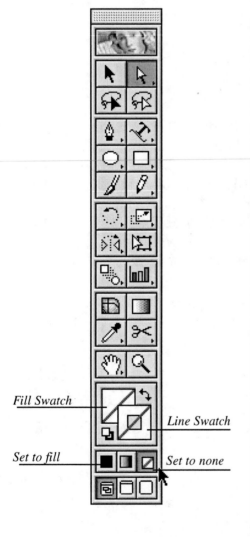

Fill Swatch

Line Swatch

Set to fill

Set to none

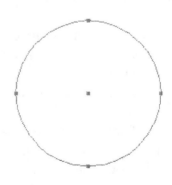

❑ Hold the mouse down on the Type tool, then select the Path Type tool from the pop-out menu, as shown to the right.

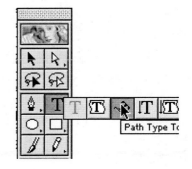

❑ Click on the circle to set the insertion point and type in some text, as shown below.

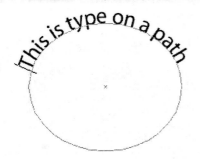

There are a huge number of effects that we could apply to this type but for this demo we'll keep it simple.

❑ Choose the selection tool from the tool palette, and click on the type to make it active.

❑ Choose File-Export to display the export dialog box.

❑ Select the Flash (SWF) format from the Format options.

ILLUSTRATOR EXPORT OPTIONS

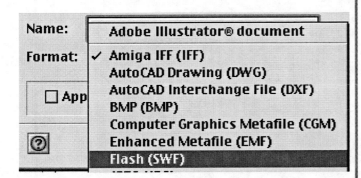

❑ Select your save location and name the file, then select the Export button to view the options.

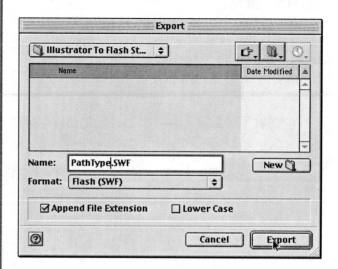

You may want to experiment with the export options depending on the artwork you're exporting. The following page provides some suggestions for selecting Export & Image Options.

SWF FORMAT DIALOG

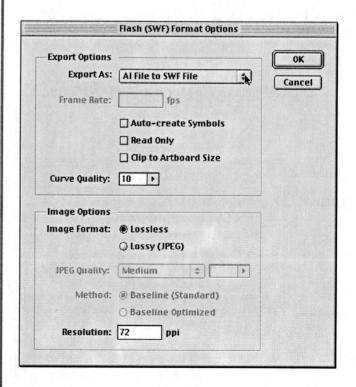

I generally leave the Auto Create Symbols option off. Once the artwork is in Flash I prefer to have an opportunity to fine tune my artwork before creating the symbol. You may feel otherwise so do not hesitate to experiment with this option. I also like to crank the curve quality to the maximum setting of ten.

Illustrator is an interesting application. It is designed to create vector images but some of the styles, on the Style palette, and some of the filters, under the Filter menu, will convert your image into a bitmap or combine bitmapped information with vector in order to produce the desired effect. While this is not ideal for Flash, some of the options, such as blur, cannot be accomplished in vector format. Fortunately Illustrator provides some accommodation in the Image Options portion of the export dialog.

Image Options: The Image Options, allows you to compress the file, if parts of it have been converted to bitmap. The text on a path image we just created will not contain any bitmapped information, so the image options with this graphic, are not important.

In addition to exporting your images, you should always save a copy of the original Illustrator source file in the event you need to make changes or try other export options.

❑ To import the file launch Flash, choose File-Import and select the file you exported from Illustrator.

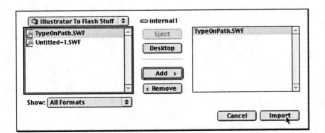

EXPORT OPTIONS

IMAGE OPTIONS

IMPORTING ILLUSTRATOR INTO FLASH

❑ To convert the graphic into a symbol, simply drag around the graphic with the pointer tool and select it, then choose Insert-Convert to Symbol.

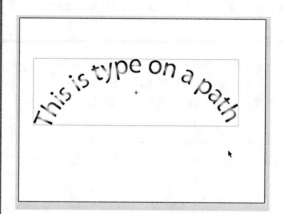

FURTHER EXPLORATION:

Further Exploration:

❑ Experiment with some of the different Styles, Strokes and Fills, found in Illustrator, to see what types of effects you can create with your type.

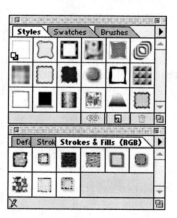

CHAPTER 32

Final Tips & Suggestions

If you have worked your way through this book then you are well on your way to becoming a Flash GURU.

In the first chapter I suggested that it is easier to learn what Flash can do before trying to implement more complex ideas. By now, you have a solid understanding of Flash. There is still a lot to learn such as more in-depth ActionScript, and there are still a few features that were not explored in this text. But, by now, you have a pretty good idea of how flash operates. You are ready for the complex projects.

Here are a couple of suggestions for tackling Flash projects.

1. Design before you develop
Before diving into a Flash project it is helpful to diagram what you want to do. It is tempting to begin the development process in Flash but you will find that larger projects can easily become pretty confusing and messy. Creating diagrams, story boards, or thumbnail sketches, before you start can help to eliminate a lot of the frustration that can occur when creating a large project.

Topics

HANDLING BIG PROJECTS 193
FURTHER READING 195
THE COMMUNICATION REVOLUTION 196

HANDLING BIG PROJECTS

2. Create Modular Objects

When you approach a large project (or even smaller projects) think in terms of individual objects. For example, if one part of your project has three different animation's occurring simultaneously, develop each animation as a separate movieclip. There are a couple of advantages to creating individual movieclips as opposed to throwing everything into one large timeline.

a. It allows you an opportunity to focus on one specific part of the final project.

b. The movieclip objects become reusable. This can save a huge amount of time for future projects.

c. The final project becomes much cleaner and easier to manage.

d. If one of the objects is not working properly, you can focus on repairing it, as opposed to tearing apart a large elaborate timeline and risking altering the function of other parts.

3. Break large ideas into the smallest component then look for the simplest solution.

I had a student who came up with this wonderful idea of allowing the user to "Erase" on a black and white image to reveal the same image in color beneath. After coming up with the idea, the next step is to think about how this can most easily be achieved. Ideally, one simple movieclip that can be used repeatedly and placed on top of both images to slowly reveal from black and white to color is the best solution.

4. Test and experiment before you commit

Using the eraser example from above, rather than working on the final erase project, experiment with simple movieclips. See if you can develop a solution in one small instance. If you can develop a single instance then it becomes the prototype for the final movieclip.

Where do you go from here?

One option is Macromedia Director. Director has many capabilities that will never be implemented in Flash. You can import your Flash animations into Director and it can both play and control a Flash animation. While Flash has great capabilities Director can do even more. Rather than providing a lengthy list I'll provide a couple of examples. In Director you can create and customize a chat room. Develop an online paint application. Develop sophisticated web games. Director 8.5 just came out with the capability to create online interactive virtual worlds (VR). Director has a steep learning curve but with your knowledge of Flash, you will find the application to be much easier to learn.

As an alternative you might be interested in further exploring Flash. More specifically learning the ActionScript language. If you are interested in programming, then ActionScript is a nice place to start. ActionScript is similar to JavaScript and also Visual Basic, but you will find the majority of the concepts and some of the structure is similar to C, C++, and Java as well as other languages. The advantage of working with Flash and ActionScript is that you get to work in a graphical environment as opposed to spending all of your time simply entering code.

By the time you read this book I'm sure there will be a variety of new books out there on ActionScript. But here are a couple of books that might interest you.

If you are familiar with programming or even if your are not but you love games. Macromedia Flash 5 ActionScript for Fun and Games, by Gary Rosenzweig is a wonderful book. Even if you only read chapters 3-5 you will have more than doubled your initial 45.00 investment. Gary writes like a true educator providing short clips of code that you can (and will want to) try immediately. The added benefit with his book is that you not only learn how to write solid code in Flash, but you get to create interesting Web games while learning.

FURTHER READING

If you want to learn programming but have no prior experience another book my students brought to my attention is Foundation ActionScript by Sham Bhangal. When students get excited about a book that says something.

A couple of other books I have recently come across that I enjoy.

ActionScripting in Flash by Phillip Kerman. It offers solid Flash programming advice and ideas. You can tell that this author knows his stuff.

Advanced Flash 5 ActionScript in Action by Dan Livingston has a huge ActionScript reference section, which is always needed and goes so far as to discuss using XML with Flash.

To really gain skills with ActionScript I actually recommend that you start building a library of reference books. When you are stuck on a problem it is always nice to have a couple of resources available for ideas and inspiration.

THE COMMUNICATION REVOLUTION

Closing Comments and hopefully some Flash inspiration:
Where you take Flash from here is something that cannot be captured in a step by step book. It involves taking your knowledge of the Flash application, and combining that knowledge with your own imagination, creativity, and new ideas. Flash is a new application and creating the kind of animated visual content that Flash can create, has only been around for a few years. Every month I encounter a new site that is not only captivating but I find myself asking either "how did they do that?" or "how did they come up with that idea!?"

The internet and applications like Flash represent the New Revolution in Communication:
If you go back in history you will find that we humans have made many attempts to convey our thoughts, ideas and emotions. Cave Paintings and tribal music were the beginnings. To this day artists

are still trying to perfect and capture something on canvas, that has never before been seen, or to capture it in a way that moves us as never before.

The written word and the printing press are regarded as revolutionary breakthroughs. The ability to mass produce text opened the door to communicate with a global population, or at least those who could read the authors language. To this day writers are still trying to perfect and explore the art of the written word. Have you ever read a book that made you laugh or touched your heart?

Then came radio, movies, and television. I don't need to mention the tremendous impact these technologies have on society. I'm sure everyone has heard a song, or seen a movie that moved them.

Applications like Flash, used on the internet, offer the same capabilities as all of these previous technologies, but also something more. Flash allows us to describe thoughts and emotions, just as with a written book, it allows us to provide movement and animation just as in a movie, and it allows us to incorporate music in new and interesting ways. But Flash offers something new, that has never been available before. You may already know the answer.

Flash allows us to create an interactive environment and make it available to a worldwide audience. No longer is the viewer resigned to the role of couch potato. They can become a part of the experience.

Artists and writers have spent centuries exploring their medium and are still finding new directions. Radio and Video have only had decades and are still in their youth as far as exploring the capabilities of their medium. But you, as a Flash developer have the distinct privilege of being one of the first to explore this breakthrough in communications.

INDEX

Hey!! What happened to the index?

A hands on training book does not readily lend itself to an index. Instead we have provided and extensive Table of Contents in the first few pages of this book.

Condensed Table of Contents

Condensed Table of Contents
First there is the condensed Table of Contents which provides a quick reference to the sections and chapters.

Chapter Topic Search

For example if you were seeking information on buttons or movieclips you can quickly locate the section and chapters that cover these topics. The first chapter in each section provides the most basic information and subsequent chapters, in the section, provide additional features or creative ideas.

Main Table of Contents

Main Table of Contents
The margin notes are referenced in the Main Table of Contents so you will find detailed page by page information.

Keyword Topic Search

Converting an Object into a Button Symbol 69
Entering the Button Symbol Editor 70
Flash Button States 70
Adding a Blank Keyframe to Button States 71
Testing the Button 71
Creating an Over State. 71
Creating a Down State. 72
Adding a Keyframes to Create Button States .. 72

For example, if you are seeking information on setting button states. By going to the section on buttons and glancing at the chapters on buttons, you will see that button states are covered on pages 70-72. Additionally you can see that page 69 discusses creating a button symbol, and page 70 discusses how to enter the symbol editor.

I hope you will find this reference useful.